The
GRANITE KISS

With many thanks and best wishes to the Sandown Public Library—

Kevin Gardner
November 14, 2012

The
GRANITE KISS

Traditions and Techniques of Building New England Stone Walls

KEVIN GARDNER

ILLUSTRATIONS BY GUILLERMO NUÑEZ

FOREWORD BY SUSAN ALLPORT

THE COUNTRYMAN PRESS

Woodstock, Vermont

Library of Congress Cataloging-in-Publication Data
Gardner, Kevin.
   The granite kiss : traditions and techniques of building New England stone walls / Kevin Gardner ; illustrations by Guillermo Nuñez ; foreword by Susan Allport.—1st ed.
     p. cm.
Includes bibliographical references and index.
ISBN 0-88150-506-4 (alk. paper)
ISBN 0-88150-546-3 (paperback)
   1. Stone walls—New England. 2. Granite. 3. Landscape construction. I. Title.

TH2249 .G38 2001
693'.1—dc21   2001037151

Cover and interior design by Trina Stahl
Cover photograph © David Brownell
Interior illustrations by Guillermo Nuñez

Published by The Countryman Press, P.O. Box 748, Woodstock, Vermont 05091
Distributed by W. W. Norton & Company, Inc., 500 Fifth Avenue, New York, NY 10110

Printed in the United States of America
10 9 8 7 6 5 4

For my mother, Penelope Owen Gardner, and, of course, for Derek

THE GRANITE KISS: *That instantly discouraging, and inevitable, experience in stone work when a fingertip or two fails to escape the contact point between two large stones on the occasion of their first meeting.*

Contents

FOREWORD

In my book *Sermons in Stone* I wrote about the many ironies surrounding the stone walls of New England and New York. The fact, for instance, that the small, walled fields created by the farmers of the eighteenth century were too small to allow farmers of the nineteenth century to use their new and more efficient farm machinery. So that stone walls, which were built by farmers at great expense in time and labor, contributed to the end of farming in the Northeast.

But there was one irony I didn't mention, one that is very immediate and pressing and raises the question of how long stone walls will continue to be a part of the New England landscape. For at the same time that our appreciation, our near reverence, for these once pragmatic structures is increasing, we are becoming increasingly out of touch with the techniques necessary to build and repair them. While we have come to value old stone walls for their visual, historical, and architectural interest, we are also in danger of losing them through active threats such as development, road projects, and pilferage, and through such passive threats as neglect.

We are drawn to stone walls in part because of their quality of seeming endurance. Stone walls, after all, are some of the only structures still remaining from the period when New England was a region of small family farms. They are some of our only reminders of a time when sheep and cattle traveled our roads, not SUVs. A time when revolutionary soldiers used stone walls as bunkers and farmers believed that small, walled fields produced best. A time, long before the estates of yesterday and today, when farmers scratched a living out of these rocky soils.

But stone walls aren't as enduring as they look. Compression and frost heaves play havoc with their shape, and vibrations from heavy trucks send stones toppling off their tops. Falling branches and leaping deer knock out entire sections, and vines and brush can pull a wall apart as effectively as any thief. Eighteenth- and nineteenth-century farmers were well aware of the relative fragility of walls, which is why they had a springtime tradition of "picking up their walls" or "mending fence" as Robert Frost described in his poem "Mending Wall." It is a tradition almost as old as wall building itself, but one that has been disregarded in most of New York and New England in the century since walls have lost their practical raison d'être. While it is encouraging that many towns in New England and New York have passed ordinances that forbid moving, removing, and/or stealing stone walls, no town, so far, has passed an ordinance requiring that existing walls be regularly maintained. And no wonder. Most homeowners wouldn't know how to go about it, and hiring an outside wall builder could be prohibitively expensive.

Happily, then, for all of us who appreciate the silent beauty of stone walls and their ability to remind us, *sic transit gloria*, of our agricultural past, Kevin Gardner has written *The Granite Kiss*, an engaging, often poetic distillation of his family's thirty years of wall-building experience that will encourage many neophytes to try their hand at this ancient, but fundamentally simple, craft.

Primers on wall building have certainly been written before, but this is the only one I know of that talks as much about stone, and gravity, and the practice of wall building, as it does about specific techniques, information that will greatly shorten the learning curve for would-be builders. The particular value of *The Granite Kiss* is that it puts readers in the right frame of mind for wall building; it gives them a way to think about stone. Nor is its usefulness limited to those it inspires to pick up a crowbar and stone hammer. Rather, this is a book that could be read by builders and armchair builders alike, by homeowners who are thinking about having a wall built or repaired, and by stone wall aficionados who wish to better understand them. Chapters on faces and placement solve the mystery of why some walls endure and others are doomed to failure, while the chapter on repair and restoration offers approaches to walls in disrepair that don't involve a complete and expensive rebuild.

Kevin Gardner's extended family of wall builders, which includes his uncle Derek Owen and sister-in-law Stephanie Gardner, also has a practical, unpretentious approach to the preservation of old walls that resonates with the annual tradition of fence mending in this country. It also resonates with my contention that few walls are of inherent historic importance, and that few walls are works of beauty in and of themselves. Gardner's aim is to restore the purpose and presence of the older wall, but to avoid the precious and precise mummification that would make preservation prohibitively expensive for most walls.

With this sensible, encouraging approach, with tips and techniques that greatly simplify and demystify wall building, *The Granite Kiss* makes the future of many walls more likely. And this should be gratifying to everyone who loves stone walls, to historians and ordinary wall watchers alike. For just as a wall is made up of many stones, so our sense of the historic and aesthetic value of walls is made up of many walls.

—SUSAN ALLPORT,
AUTHOR OF *Sermons in Stone:
The Stone Walls of New England
and New York*

ACKNOWLEDGMENTS

ALTHOUGH I SET down the words in this book, I am in no true sense its only author. The material in *The Granite Kiss* is in many ways the record of a long collaboration among the wall-building members of my family, including my sister-in-law Stephanie, my brother Chris, his former wife, Christine, my aunt Ruth, and, of course, my uncle Derek. All of them, and others who have worked with us, have contributed techniques, insights, and even the vocabulary that define this book's approach and form its structure. *The Granite Kiss* would have no reason to exist if not for them.

I am impossibly indebted to two other family members as well: to Bill Nuñez, a superb artist long before he became my brother-in-law, whose beautiful drawings lend these pages grace and clarity they would not otherwise have had; and to my wife's father, Admiral S. Robert Foley Jr., USN, who read the manuscript on an ongoing basis and whose support, insights, and encouragement can never be repaid.

My warmest thanks to Susan Allport, not only for her great generosity in contributing the foreword to this book, but also for her own marvelous work, *Sermons in Stone*, which has been our continuous resource, and a parting gift for our clients, since it first appeared more than ten years ago.

I am also grateful to Scott Swank, of Canterbury Shaker Village, for his willingness to share both his knowledge and the village's archival photographs, and to Tom Wessels, author of *Reading the Forested Landscape*, for his expertise on the demise of the American chestnut.

The University of Connecticut's Dr. Robert Thorson, an imaginative geologist and the author, with his wife, Kristine, of the award-winning (and perhaps only) children's book about walls, the delightful *Stone Wall Secrets*, gave me timely and generous assistance with the details of New England's geological history.

More broadly, I have learned a great deal over the years in conversations with several distinguished New England historians, among them David Watters, of the University of New Hampshire; Jere Daniell, of Dartmouth College; R. Stuart Wallace, of Plymouth State College; and Steve Taylor, commissioner of New Hampshire's Department of Agriculture, Markets, and Food. Their enormous knowledge of New England's history and landscape has found its way into nearly every cranny of *The Granite Kiss*, although, I rush to add, any misstatements or misinterpretations of historical matters here must be attributed to me, not them.

I am delighted to have the chance to thank New Hampshire Public

Radio and its president, Mark Handley, for sixteen years' worth of benign endurance of my sometimes peculiar interpretation of the word *deadline*, and for the fascinating opportunities the station has given me to travel around New Hampshire and New England, and to interview so many of the region's finest writers, artists, and thinkers. The New Hampshire Humanities Council has also contributed significantly to these opportunities.

The Granite Kiss has had the indescribably beneficent fortune to have passed, in manuscript, through the hands of playwright and teacher A. R. Gurney Jr., architectural historian Jim Garvin, of the New Hampshire Office of Historic Preservation, and the writer Howard Mansfield. Mere public acknowledgment seems a paltry way of thanking them for their numerous and astute comments, corrections, and literary midwifery—it would be far more appropriate to go straight to their homes and build as many walls as they like, so valuable have their insights and wisdom been.

The gracious professionalism of Ann Kraybill, Jennifer Thompson, and others at The Countryman Press has been a continuing pleasure, and I feel extremely fortunate to have had their guidance and assistance.

Finally, a kiss of gratitude (not granite) to my wife (and most vigilant editor), Brenda Foley, the author of everything good in our small, wooded corner of the world, whose faith and love are stronger than stone.

DEREK OWEN
Derek Owen stands at the base of a retaining wall built around a large culvert. Near the top of the wall, to his right, the face shows a crossed T, one of his stylistic trademarks. (After a photograph by Timothy Savard.)

INTRODUCTION

THIS IS A book about building stone walls and about the values we attach to them. It describes traditional techniques of dry stone construction as practiced and preserved by my uncle, Derek Owen, of Hopkinton, New Hampshire, and other members of our family. For almost thirty years we have worked together building and restoring stone walls in the New England style, and teaching the craft and its history in workshops, demonstrations, and lectures. *The Granite Kiss* combines lessons we have taught with those we have learned and explores the fascination we, and many others, feel for this most expedient and humble art.

A considerable renaissance in the profession of stone wall building has taken place during the years we've been in business, but unlike many other specialized trades, dry stone construction is something almost anyone can do. Its principles are not complex (although they must be practiced), and it requires few tools homeowners do not already have. Wall building's physical demands, while not insignificant, are much less daunting than its reputation suggests. As Curtis Fields observed in his 1971 book, *The Forgotten Art of Building a Stone Wall*, "I have learned that it is not brawn that is needed so much as a basic understanding of the laws of physics." Beyond this, wall building is a surprisingly personal activity, something no two people do precisely the same way. This is part of the reason it is so satisfying—for some—to learn.

The Granite Kiss is by no means a comprehensive instruction manual for masons, however. It concentrates almost entirely on the phenomenon of the New England stone wall, an unmortared icon chiefly distinguished by adaptability and lack of pretense. For something so celebrated, New England walls are remarkably ordinary creations. Irish stone walls are more artful, and Italian ones more elegant. The ancient assemblages of the Middle East are more venerable, and the astonishing works of the Egyptians and the Mayans more precise. The nineteenth-century explosion of wall building in the English countryside created a nearly unrivaled spectacle of mortarless masonry. Compared with other wonders of the dry-stone world, New England walls are almost laughably runtish, and they are as recent as they are primitive— the oldest verifiable standing wall in New England cannot have been erected much longer than 350 years ago, whereas in Ireland alone the tradition is traceable over 5,000 years.

Nevertheless, in terms of sheer bulk and extent, and as representatives of the potential of communal hand labor, the stone walls of New

England collectively rank among the great architectural accomplishments of history. What they lack in pedigree they make up in impact, both physically, as features of the landscape, and culturally, as signifiers of place and tradition. *The Granite Kiss* is interested in the lingering effects of that tradition, as felt by those who take it into their heads to build stone walls today.

Still, this is not a book of history. Susan Allport has already written that book, and her *Sermons in Stone* contains much of the factual research buried in the base of *The Granite Kiss*. For those who want a thoroughgoing exploration of the historical origins and significance of New England stone walls, Allport's book is the only place to go.

The Granite Kiss is about New England stone walls today: how to build them, why people wish to build them, and what can be done with them. Because a great deal of the skill of wall building is actually about seeing, this book discusses ways to evaluate both the place where your wall might stand and the individual stones you select as you build. There are tips on design, on site preparation, and on procurement of materials, as well as the essential arts of placement and fitting. There is reassurance about the availability of this skill to any reasonably able-bodied person who might want to learn it. There is rumination on the paradoxical mythology of New England walls, which simultaneously attracts would-be builders and intimidates them. There is a chapter on the things that make walls beautiful.

Above all, this book's advice is intended to be practical, grounded in the knowledge that New England wall builders must inevitably contend with shapes and types of stone that are, to put it mildly, less than ideal for easy dry construction. Random, rounded fieldstone is the rule rather than the exception in much of glacier-scoured New England, so the techniques I describe are meant to help builders make the best possible use of stone that the fussier masons of more sophisticated traditions would find unacceptable (and the writers of more glibly optimistic instruction manuals would prefer to ignore). Very little study of the walls and other dry stone structures of New England's past is required to see that their builders were often far less concerned with presenting perfect-looking monuments than with making effective and lasting use of the stone they had at hand. The Owen family's orientation is similar to theirs. Our stones are theirs.

In some cases, however, our terminology is our own. *The Granite Kiss*, for better or worse, freely employs idiosyncratic words, phrases, and metaphors developed as a kind of communicative shorthand during our family's years of working together. So, mixed in with the standard vocabulary of masonry—words like *course*, *face*, *capstone*, and *battered*—readers will encounter some decidedly more eccentric terms, such as *thrufter*, *dinner plate*, *cantaloupe*, and *cheap seducer*, words that, however unlikely they are to find places in the lexicon of the trade, have served us too habitually and conveniently to be discarded now. The book's title, in fact, is one of these phrases: It refers to the delightful experience of getting your fingertips crushed between stones. To avoid subjecting readers to future conversational embarrassment, and the blank stares of masons who have never heard of *cat caves* and *problem-*

solvers, I have distinguished the Owen coinages from more conventional language, both in the text and in the section titled "Our Glossary." All glossary terms, whether unique to our family or enshrined in common usage, are italicized upon first mention in the text.

With or without customized terminology, however, learning to build stone walls is not like learning Latin, the cello, or horseshoeing. Beyond certain fundamental structural principles, traditional New England stone work is by its nature a self-taught skill, subject to technical and aesthetic variations as infinite as snowflakes. For this reason, the instructional literature of wall building, sound as it may be, has only limited value. Furthermore, in Susan Allport's words, ". . . when it comes time to offer practical advice on how best to build a stone wall, these publications, curiously enough, almost always disagree in nearly every aspect of construction." Allport is not speaking here of the dozen or so contemporary books on wall building, although she might as well be, but of agricultural journals and manuals issued in the early and middle years of the nineteenth century, when dry masonry was far more widely practiced than it is today. The fact that the chroniclers of the craft could not get their story straight even at the peak of its development only underscores the individual nature of any given builder's approach to the task.

The Granite Kiss, therefore, is not a book that seeks to dictate every stage of your wall building with step-by-step instruction. Rather, it is a book of principles and practices, adaptable techniques and effective working methods, tricks to remember and traps to avoid. Far from the last word on how to build in unmortared stone, it is in fact a kind of *first* word, for beginners or experimenters, simply a starting point for anyone who ever wondered if this ancient traditional craft might be worth a try. New England stone walls are more than quaint anachronisms or regional emblems. For those who learn something about building them, stone walls are also historical documents, personal statements, and uniquely engaging activity. They are what landscape historian J. B. Jackson called "history as the chronicle of everyday existence," and their building teaches lessons about the past, the present, and the self in ways few other kinds of "everyday" work can match.

The
GRANITE KISS

A SINGLE-STACK WALL
AGAINST WOODS
The simple single-stack wall is now rarely built, but still ubiquitous around New England's fields and forests. This one needs some experienced attention.

MYTH *and* PARADOX

HISTORICAL CONTEXTS AND MISCONCEPTIONS THAT INFLUENCE STONE WALL BUILDERS TODAY

To see the ghostly outline of an old landscape beneath the superficial cover-ing of the contemporary is to be made vividly aware of the endurance of core myths.

—SIMON SCHAMA, *Landscape and Memory*

Look on my works, ye Mighty, and despair!

—PERCY BYSSHE SHELLEY, "Ozymandias"

THE RENOWN OF the New England stone wall draws nourishment from three principal myths: of silence, of permanence, and of craft. The myth of silence endows an old wall with dignity bordering on the mysterious, mutely proclaiming the stupendous tedium of hand labor endured by its creators and celebrating their stoic, ephemeral victory over the wilderness. The myth of permanence proclaims that their work stands forever as first constructed, mossily demonstrating an integrity our own age long ago mislaid. As for craft, it is commonly believed that antique stone walls are the masterpieces of a vanished race of masonic savants whose secrets lie with them today under rows of slate and marble headstones in overgrown country cemeteries. Paradoxically, each of these myths contains just enough truth to sustain itself in popular imagination and just enough untruth to inhibit genuine understanding. The complex fascination New England stone walls seem to inspire in so many people arises from the tension between the objects themselves, which are serene, enduring, and finished, and our perceptions of them, which are dissatisfied, volatile, and evolving.

These perceptions account for much of the admiration and nostalgia that attach themselves, like flat blooms of lichen, to the miles of old stone walls that still remain, but they are not much help to anyone who wants to learn to build in stone today. They are, in a way, as obstructive as the stones themselves once were to the generations of farmers who struggled so relentlessly to evict them from croplands and pastures. Still, respect for the efforts of New England's original wall builders is by no means inappropriate. As Susan Allport points out, the achievement represented by New England's thousands of miles of stone walls compares more than favorably with the construction of the pyramids of Egypt. Extrapolating from an estimate made by naturalist Edwin Way Teale and an 1871 report of the United States Department of Agriculture, she writes, "It would have taken . . . 15,000 men [working 365 days a year] 243 years to build the 252,539 miles of walls in New England and New York." These astonishing numbers assume even greater significance in light of two other facts: The entire nation of Great Britain, where dry walling began much sooner, and lasted longer, contains only about 70,000 miles of stone walls. And Allport's figures refer only to walls—they do not include innumerable dry stone constructions such as foundations, ramps, stairways, wells, and bridges.

Even so, the laborious heroism of our forebears need not be elevated to mythological status in order for us to honor their accomplishment. For them, wall building was ordinary work. And so it is for us. To begin, we must set aside just a little of the mythology and see the job for what it is: a task with steps and rules and predictable outcomes.

THE MYTH OF SILENCE

MY UNCLE DEREK says that he can hear stones speak, even call to him as he rummages through some old crumbled wall or farmer's stone-dump on a search for special shapes. His hearing is enhanced by humorous mysticism and the anthropomorphic respect most crafts-people develop for their materials, but it is also practical. For stones *do* speak with individual voices, from the tight ceramic clink of flat, thin *dinner plates* to the compressive basso tap of two-hundred-pound granite *cannonballs*. *Sandstone* whispers and grinds, rotten *shale* knocks hollowly and falls apart, small mobs of field-picked pebbles rush from the breach in a pasture wall with a burst of energetic gossip.

Derek's fifty years of manual and auditory intimacy with New England fieldstone have taught him to separate the voices of individual stones, one from another. And his eye, measuring and appreciating a long run of old, well-laid wall, sees not only its massed coherence, its entirety, but also its single members, their types and shapes, the mixture of sizes, their characteristic relationships, their flaws. These and other evidentiary convergences of accident and intent are apparent to him in places where others see only an outline, a boundary, a rambling barrier identical to countless others. Derek's understanding of how walls work, and of the clues that may reveal something about a long-gone builder, breaks the silence of antique walls and gives them voices, too; voices that are almost as likely to speak of haste, revision, or carelessness as of circumspection, planning, and skill.

The Myth of Permanence

IN THE HUMAN scheme of things, the idea of permanence is something of a conceit. Stone walls, for reasons that perhaps have more to do with our need to hold on to our veneration for our ancestors than with the walls' actual longevity, have become the beneficiaries of a kind of longing for a purer time. They have come to symbolize certain values we fervently desire to be enduring. Their apparent permanence, then, is more a matter of cultural and emotional transference than of genuine immutability.

In fact, most of New England's old stone walls lie in states of disrepair that would render them unrecognizable to their original builders, but the power of their appeal is so great that it transcends their actual condition. As contemporary wall builders, we regularly find ourselves asked to duplicate the tumbled wreckage of unmaintained antique walls, not because our customers consciously wish to landscape their properties with ruins, but because the imagery of ruined walls is more familiar and therefore more "authentic" than the tighter, taller look of something new. Lovers of antique things can accept and even appreciate a certain level of distress in the objects they admire, but where stone walls are concerned, this expectation has been developed to the point of stylistic preference. Why this should be so is not entirely clear. In many New England towns, stone walls are not even the oldest extant structures to be found. Particularly in long-settled coastal communities or in old villages along the rivers, there are often wooden buildings considerably older than any wall to be found in the area. Yet our attachment to stonework as a primary metaphor of endurance persists. Perhaps that is because stone walls, more than any other human structures, are a nearly perfect marriage of natural occurrence and human artifice. Their permanence belongs not so much to themselves as it does to our ideas of this ancient earth and our own fragile tenure on its crust.

THE MYTH OF CRAFT

THERE IS NO question that many examples of old stonework display extraordinary combinations of engineering intelligence and artistic sensitivity. The town pounds in places like Lyndeborough, New Hampshire, and Waldoboro, Maine; numerous cemetery walls throughout

New England; and countless milldams, livestock runs, barn foundations, and even humble *single-stack walls* still contain intact sections and occasional lengthy stretches of beautifully fitted stone. Fragmentary instances of near perfection in both design and execution can be found in many places.

Nevertheless, the notion that all, or even most, of the old stonework we see around New England is the result of a concentrated application of arcane skill is demonstrably false. This idea has taken hold in part because of our wonderment at the incomprehensible amount of drudgery undertaken by the families who settled here in the seventeenth and eighteenth centuries. How could anything so difficult be done carelessly or badly? A second influence is simple longevity. Since good walls last longer than bad ones, what we see around us today, at a 175-year remove from the end of the period of their most prolific construction, is more likely than not to be among the best work ever laid down. The third reason is the plainest of all: In a contemporary society that hardly values and rarely practices manual agricultural arts, most of us have no way of distinguishing between excellence and indifference in traditional dry masonry. Therefore, we honor the builders of the past with our admiration for everything they left behind, regardless of its actual quality. In light of the degree to which the myth of craft prevents some would-be wall builders from learning this ancient skill, however, a brief historical review may provide a little reassurance. How did we get all these walls, anyway?

Following this exceedingly laborious toil [cutting down the forest] came not only the difficult task of plowing and planting, but the almost endless labor of removing the rocks and stones that thickly cumbered the surface of the ground. Stones were utilized in the division of lots by walls, which were often thick, or double . . . Heaps of stone thrown up in waste places are significant monuments of the severe toil through which the early inhabitants of this town reclaimed the wilderness.

—CHARLES CHASE LORD, *Life and Times in Hopkinton, N.H.*

On a certain road near Washington, New Hampshire—a beautiful little hill town not terribly near any major highway—a glance into the woods will give you some idea of what the earliest European settlers faced when they set about the task of converting the land into farms. The ground is so littered with stones of every size, from baseballs to bushel baskets to Volkswagen-sized boulders, that the very idea of trying to convert it to cropland or pasture resembles an act of desperation or insanity. Yet land like this is precisely what New England's original wall builders confronted. For them, craftsmanship as a general rule of wall construction took second place, if that, to the much greater necessity of moving all that rubble out of the way. The indignation of romantic post-Colonialists notwithstanding, it is more than likely that many miles of today's tumbled, moundlike walls, especially in outlying areas long abandoned to reforestation, have not changed very much

MILLRACE RUIN

*The ruins of an ancient millrace in Hopkinton, New Hampshire,
stand more than nine feet tall. These rough-cut blocks were most
likely laid by professionals working with oxen, tripods, and heavy
gin-poles. The dam, which runs off to the right, is more than ten feet
thick and entirely built of laid stone.*

structurally but have only been slowly buried in leaf mold and accumulations of forest trash. These walls, unlike more public projects meant to express the achievements and prosperity of whole communities, were never intended to showcase any sort of craftsmanship. Many were not even assembled as "walls" at all but dumped or tossed underneath zigzag split rail fencing that has long since rotted away.

Between these two extremes—rambling collections of unsorted rubble thrown into loose mounds, and the most finely assembled formal public projects—a host of styles and degrees of expertise was brought to the task of suppressing New England's random riot of scattered stone. Even the remnants of that work, whatever their condition today, provide evidence that nothing like a unified commitment to craft was in force during the creation of the region's vast network of walls. Like any other common job, wall building had its geniuses and its dunces, and in between, an enormous middle group of practitioners who knew the basics of the task but regarded it as a chore, not a craft. If their finest work looks better than our own today, it is at least partly because they had more time to practice and more pressing reasons to do so. Thanks to them, we can plant gardens or stroll through the woods on thousands of New England acres without stumbling over the uncountable glacial tonnage they spent large portions of their lives storing in walls. This is perhaps the most undervalued of their legacies, for New England's farmer-builders also left behind a vivid model of the relationship between life and landscape, one whose appeal seems only to grow as the time of its actuality recedes further and further into the past.

All around them in this rocky town, and in hundreds of very similar New England communities, there evolved and briefly flourished a nearly finished way of life, a self-sufficient agriculture . . . intimately tied to cultivating the resistant land and harvesting its forest.

— RONALD JAGER, *Last House on the Road*

New England stone walls are encrusted with contradiction. It is not the least of their ironies that these symbols of endurance and stability were erected, historically speaking, in something of a rush: One estimate finds that the majority of the region's walls were built between 1775 and 1825, a mere fifty years. Another, even briefer estimate places a peak period of construction from 1810 to 1840, a minute interval for so profound a mark on the landscape. Certainly, the practicality of building fences out of stone appealed to people living necessarily frugal lives in a country strewn with glacial rubble. But stone was not their first choice of fencing material: Widespread use of it began only when other alternatives—stumps and split rails—grew scarce because of overclearing. If New England's wall builders attained a kind of greatness in their work, it was a greatness that, in Shakespeare's words, was partly "thrust upon 'em."

Notwithstanding the practicalities of their origin, stone walls (like other fencing) acquired immediate symbolism as representatives of the English system of private, enclosed land ownership. This system (a relatively new one in the eighteenth century) opposed older European models first brought to America by the Puritans in which grazing and other lands were held and worked in common. Much more significantly, it also ended forever the traditional land management practices of Native Americans, whose mobile settlement patterns, diversified, non-intensive planting, and regular use of fire to clear the forest understory had, over thousands of years, helped produce the very conditions of ecological abundance and agricultural potential that attracted colonists in the first place. Historian William Cronon has amply demonstrated that the "hordes of European grazing animals" introduced into the territories of New England by white settlers, along with the fencing that contained those animals, played a fundamental role in beginning a "dynamic and unstable process of ecological change" that continues even today. In addition to their seminal contribution to New England's beloved appearance, then, stone walls also provided one of the first American examples of the unintended consequences of development.

In spite of the conflicts they embodied, and helped create, stone walls had emerged by the end of the eighteenth century as signifiers of industry, establishment, and prosperity, and their integral presence in a landscape devoted to small-scale subsistence farming seemed permanently assured. But the mid-nineteenth century's industrialization of agricultural technique transformed stone walls from ornaments to obstructions. New, horse-drawn machinery—mowers, reapers, tedders, and spreaders—needed larger spaces than the tiny, stone-enclosed plots laid out by previous generations for handwork and teams of oxen. Frustration and resentment replaced pride in New Englanders' attitude toward their walls, and this shift was aggravated by other symptoms of agricultural stagnation. The sheep industry collapsed, a victim of unstable business cycles, regional and foreign competition, and the loss of tariff protection. The thin soils of the upland grew exhausted, making many farms less and less profitable. Young people, and even whole families, migrated in large numbers to industrializing cities and the newly opened West.

The long goodbye to New England's era of small-farm dominance added a new layer of symbolism to the old stones—nostalgia. Progressive abandonment of cleared land, the disappearance of wooden structures, and the swift return of the forest left stone walls on thousands of acres the only substantial legacy of a virtual civilization that had vanished almost within living memory. The late nineteenth and early twentieth centuries saw an outpouring of emotional eulogies for the farmer-builders who had laid the walls, ranging from the sweetly sorrowful to the bitterly despondent. "Mourning New England," writer Howard Mansfield declares, "was a small industry." Although some recent scholarship, notably Hal S. Barron's study *Those Who Stayed Behind*, has argued convincingly that the region's agricultural decline was far less catastrophic in social and economic terms than contemporary accounts and conventional wisdom have suggested, there can be no doubt that this period witnessed the gradual abandonment of extensive tracts of painstakingly developed farmland, along with the walls that divided and defined it.

Amid twentieth-century struggles with war, Depression, and redevelopment, stone walls have largely been ignored or abused, thus taking on yet another qualitative aspect—irrelevance. Buried to enlarge fields, crushed up to pave new roads, or simply absorbed by the forest, New England's walls spent the first half of the century in a state somewhere between slumber and erosion, hardly noticed by a population too preoccupied to pay attention to the relics of a faded past.

But the last thirty years or so have restored their contradictory capacities, as touchstones, so to speak, of tradition and change. Enormously accelerated development pressure on the New England landscape has rediscovered stone walls in two not always compatible ways: As historical assets and as building material. Preservationists advocate for their protection on grounds that the old walls help to define New England's regional specificity and contain irreplaceable historical information, even as large and small developers continue to destroy them or recycle their stones in new construction. As it was in the beginning, the values we attach to stone walls remain a study in contradiction, so it is hardly surprising that today, as more of the old work disappears, its emblematic significance grows larger and larger. New England's traditional landscape (and its architectural legacy) have in many places succumbed to pressures that turn farmland into cluster housing, and the roads approaching towns into sprawling commercial strips. The economic vitality that such redevelopment represents might have been welcomed with wholehearted enthusiasm in other eras, but in our day such generic transformation of a once distinctive countryside is regarded by some as an assault on the region's individuality. We live in a period of accelerating unease in which the world around us shifts and reconfigures itself almost weekly, and the forces that seem to spin it faster and faster operate from great distances, unaffected and frequently undeterred by local desires or considerations.

In such a context New England's stone walls have attracted renewed interest and admiration in several ways. Stone walls are indisputably local, far more explicit as expressions of place and culture than almost anything else we build. They represent a constancy we find in short supply these days (notwithstanding their advancing deterioration and, in some areas, outright disappearance), and they have become the most ubiquitous reminder of a former New England, which even our unsentimental age regards with a certain wistfulness. "I think this kind of monument is celebrating a different past," said landscape historian J. B. Jackson, "not the past which history books describe, but a vernacular past, a golden age where there are no dates or names, simply a sense of the way it *used to be*, history as the chronicle of everyday existence." Today, the impact of our old stone walls, as familiar framing structures for the increasingly precious rural landscape, is perhaps more profound than ever, given the erosion of so many of that landscape's other signifying features; its open, cleared space, separated farmsteads, and well-defined villages. The tangible simplicity of stone walls appeals to people whose working lives are characterized by the abstract complexities of the information age, whether they are moved to learn the craft themselves or only to see it preserved. Moreover, New England stone walls have arrived at a time in their history when, in spite of their apparent anachronism, they are entering a period of renewal and reconsideration that is, in yet another paradox, at least partly a *result* of their long twentieth-century slumber. As Jackson puts it, "there has to be that interval of neglect, there has to be discontinuity; it is religiously and artistically essential. That is what I mean when I refer to the necessity for ruins: ruins provide the incentive for restoration, and for a return to origins. There has to be (in our new concept of history) an interim of death or rejection before there can be renewal or reform."

By just about any reasonable measure, J. B. Jackson's "interval of neglect" has long since run its course where New England's stone walls are concerned. A rebirth of active attention to the craft and its many uses, then, is in some sense overdue. But our new interest in stone walls also expresses a certain kind of continuity—the stones, after all, are still here—and the glimmering of a larger awareness; that preservation of a regional landscape's identifying features can be an active, not merely curatorial process. Perhaps this is why we have encountered so much enthusiasm among our students, who seem to take delight in learning a thing that is new and old at the same time, that engages them physically in ways that are challenging but not insurmountable, and that offers a kind of artistic satisfaction at once visceral and abstract.

Still, the mythologies of the New England stone wall mutter discouragement to would-be builders. They warn of mysterious lost craftsmanship, of impossible combinations of brawn and stoicism, of the superior work ethic of the dead. Whether the region's original builders would regard our intimidated veneration with amusement or disbelief is unknowable. But the truth is that almost anyone can build a stone wall, and the qualities required to do it are readily transferable from other, more familiar tasks.

If you can piece a quilt, you can build in stone. If you can stack wood, assemble a jigsaw puzzle, arrange flowers, pack a suitcase, compose a photograph, or set a nice table, you already know essential things about dry stone work. Mastery of a few basic structural details will get you started. Willingness to practice, with hands *and* eyes, will eventually endow you with real skill. The many thousands of miles of New England's old walls were not built by highly trained supermen but by ordinary farmers and workers, children, women, indentured servants, Native Americans, and slaves; people of every shape and size. The principal difference between their approach and ours is not ability but motivation. For them, walls were a practical necessity, a fundamental component of the way they organized the landscape. For us, aesthetic considerations are primary. We no longer need to dispose of large amounts of stone in order to plow or plant. We have not cleared away the available lumber so profligately that stone is all we have left for fencing. Nor can stone walls accomplish anything that can't be done more quickly and cheaply in some other way. When we build walls today, we do it for a variety of reasons that reflect everything from preservationist philosophy and artistic preference to a simple desire for the pleasures of the work. Our attitude is only the latest in a series of cultural and economic mood swings that have made New Englanders' historic relationship to their stone walls far less stable than the walls themselves. While this instability has done its share of damage, both to the walls and to the transmission of the craft, it has also enriched the mythology of New England's stone walls, helping to make them the icons they have become and contributing to a mild form of secular apotheosis of the trade's remaining (and emerging) masters—a circumstance some of us have been only too happy to exploit. In fact, the greatest contemporary contribution to the stream of paradoxes attendant on New England stone walls may well be the overscaled admiration occasionally heaped on wall builders for what, in many ways, is a relatively easy thing to do.

By no means, however, do the attractions of old New England walls and their celebrated makers spring entirely from mythology, misperception, and nostalgia. Along with its acquired reputation as a haven for the mysteriously adept, the traditional craft of wall building derives enormous inspiration from its former practitioners, whose instincts for striking yet practical design, imaginative technical acumen, and sensitivity to the potential of their materials remain, in many places, to instruct us still. Close observation of their finest extant work teaches endless lessons about the mating of shapes, the relationships between structure and landscape, and, perhaps most fundamentally, about perseverance; the appreciation that this is a job that can be done efficiently but not quickly. This instructive legacy, though much less widely heralded than wall building's mythic reputation, is available to anyone with the willingness, and the temperament, to practice and to persist.

Mythology notwithstanding, access to its assistance is not dependant on innate ability of any kind. "Talent is a word we use *after* someone has become accomplished," says renowned painter Richard Schmid. "There is no way to detect it before the fact, or when someone is still grappling with the learning process . . . It is a complex mixture of motive, curiosity, receptivity, intelligence, sensitivity, good teaching, perseverance, timing, sheer luck, and countless other things."

The "talent" for building stone walls is no more inherent in any person than the "talent" for baking cakes or fixing a car. Like those skills, it is also gender-neutral. The traditional assumption that men are somehow better suited to the craft is no more sensible than the convictions that women should not vote or drive automobiles—two other discredited absurdities that once enjoyed common currency. The stones in most ordinary New England walls average hardly more than sixty to seventy-five pounds apiece, weights most healthy people can lift with ease. Much of the stone in the vast majority of projects is even lighter than that, particularly when walls require extensive interior packing. Brute strength is certainly an asset, but a minor one, far less important than mastery of the specifics of fitting and form. In fact, if any irresponsibly general statement can be made about the suitability of either sex for the building of stone walls, it is that women are more likely to appreciate its principles and the subtleties of application that flow from them than are men. Certainly, this has been our experience at many workshops, and our own family crew has continuously operated with female members for almost twenty years. Lifting a stone is only a mechanical problem, susceptible to all kinds of mechanical solutions; knowing where to put it is something rather more complex, a skill for which biological predisposition is impossible to identify.

Women, and men, who set out to teach themselves traditional New England wall building today usually find that its myths and ironies can be sublimated but never entirely dismissed. Nor would the majority of new builders think of doing so, for the rich paradoxes of the craft are among its primary attractions. In fact, the activity of building has served for many as a unique form of understanding, a way to achieve insight as well as practical results, and to contribute to the heritage of engagement with landscape that has shaped and reshaped our region's identity for more than 350 years. To learn to build stone walls is one of the best ways of seeing how reality and cultural myth-making intersect, and to master the craft is to strike a kind of balance between the two. In the last few decades, as new waves of settlement bring about yet another transformation of the countryside, more and more New Englanders are discovering what their predecessors also learned; that the old stones they see everywhere about them are not fixed or static things but movable, mendable, and adaptable, enriching the *new* New England landscape as naturally, and paradoxically, as they helped mythologize the landscape of New England's past. This alone should be more than enough to keep the tradition alive.

BARN RAMP

The design of this typical ramp allows vehicular access to the main floor of the barn, and provides an ample track for livestock. The building's slight elevation, on uneven terrain, also exposes its lower level at the side and in back.

GETTING STARTED

2

PREPARING THE SITE, ACQUIRING MATERIAL, AND LAYING OUT THE WALL

> *If you pile one little thing on top of another, and do this often, you will soon have a heap.*
>
> —HESIOD, *Works and Days* (eighth century B.C.E.)

DRY STONE STRUCTURES CAN assume a large variety of forms, but all of them are variations on one or the other of only two essential types: the freestanding and the retainer. *Freestanding walls* rise off the ground into space and show on all sides. *Retaining walls*, or *retainers*, show on only one side and are extensions of the higher of two different ground levels that meet where the wall stands. Single-stack farmer walls, field walls, town pounds, and standard two-by-two-foot garden walls are (generally) freestanding. Any wall that holds back a bank of earth or marks an abrupt change in surface level is a retainer. Steps, wells, foundations, culvert headers, and many other structures are variations of this category. Some constructions, like ramps, causeways, and

1

bridges (and many walls, too), incorporate combinations of the free-standing and the retainer.

Why does this distinction matter? Because it has significant influence on how you go about preparing to build, as well as on techniques of building. Freestanding walls, which show twice as much face as do retainers, require fussier picking and more careful placement, particularly in the wall's interior. Retaining walls allow the disposition of larger amounts of poorly shaped stone but require more volume and often more extensive site preparation.

Getting ready to build means preparing the site and gathering stone. The most common error beginning builders make is failure to provide themselves with sufficient material. Simple multiplication can tell you roughly how much volume you will need for a project—fifty feet of two-by-two-foot garden wall, for instance, will eventually use up two hundred cubic feet, or about 11½ tons of stone. But for those who wish to combine efficiency and discrimination, merely gathering the projected finished volume will not do. We regularly haul in as much as a third more than that, just to provide ourselves with enough choices to meet the structural and aesthetic needs of the wall as it develops. By obligating yourself to use every stone at hand, you condemn your technique to degradation, as the best of your material disappears long before the project is done. Few things are as dispiriting as the hours wasted in fruitless efforts to build good walls with ugly or structurally inadequate stones. Where raw material is concerned, we have learned that hauling loads of extras away after the job is done is far more efficicnt than is pursuing a false economy of full employment. Even our illustrious ancestors wasted little time with lousy stone—our excavations of many of their mammoth discard piles have revealed that, more often than not, they consist almost entirely of useless, unbuildable junk.

Essential as they are, large stockpiles of stone only help if they include wide variations of shape and size. In work with random fieldstone, processes of assembly, as well as the finished product, are immeasurably enhanced by the broadest possible choice. Flat, thin plates, long, skinny cigars, broken triangles, elongated cubes, bushel-basket blocks, and odd, smaller shapes of every size and description are necessary not only for visual texture, but also because they make possible the secure installation of the tons of rounded glacial nondescripts that inevitably dominate any supply of New England fieldstone. In this light it is wise to pick your stone with some care, particularly if your project is relatively small, thin, or finely fitted. *Double-faced walls* require twice as many well-shaped face stones; very high retainers need a larger supply of long, or large, base stones; delicate, low garden walls may call for extra flat capping material, and so on. Willingness to pick through available stone before you commit it to the site can save enormous labor later on. Unless you are certain to have space for large amounts of undistinguished material, as in thick retainers or very wide freestanding walls, be prepared to discriminate at the source.

Locating that source is harder than it used to be, particularly if you're looking for weathered native fieldstone. If you don't happen to live on an old farm with its own supply of recyclable stone, some creativity and persistence may be necessary. It is still possible to find landowners willing to part with the tumbled walls on their back acreage, and the farther you travel from larger population centers, the easier it gets. This can mean some legwork, obviously, but asking around, locating the friend of a friend, or contacting mason contractors in outlying towns can help. Selectmen, road agents, or local excavating or land-clearing companies are also potential sources of information.

If the gods are smiling on you, you may find a supply that you can have for the hauling. More often these days, you'll have to pay for it. Stone can be sold by weight or by volume, and when the source is a landowner rather than a commercial operation, a little dickering is frequently part of the transaction. Some sellers will ask that you take entire sections of wall rather than just the stones you want, but this is not always a good idea, as you may find yourself obligated to move large amounts of material you cannot use. Take a good look at what you're buying before you agree to the deal.

How much should you pay? The answer depends on a number of factors: the quality of the stone, its accessibility, whether or not the owner is willing to help you reach it or load it, and the distance you have to travel. Whether you have your own truck or trailer, or have to hire one, is another consideration. The number of trips you have to make and the capacity of your conveyance are still others. Make a rough assessment of the time and money you will spend to deliver the amount of stone you need to your site. Then compare this cost to the commercial alternative—having a building materials supplier deliver the stone to you on pallets. Recent years have seen considerable growth in this service, but it isn't cheap. Palletized stone costs anywhere from $250 to $600 (or more) for a stack roughly 3½ feet cubed, and delivery fees are frequently added to the price. Even so, if your project isn't terribly large you may find this more practical than a foraging expedition into the countryside. There was a time when stone seekers could range around the back roads of New England and simply help themselves to any supply they happened on, but that practice is now a good way to get arrested. "Igneous larceny," in our family parlance, is one of the reasons the roadside walls in so many places are in such bad shape today.

We have paid landowners as little as $5 and as much as $40 for a ton of stone, a range of prices that should be understood more as a reflection of where we happen to be in New England than as any kind of standard. As a general rule, the farther north or into the hinterlands you travel, the more likely you are to find reasonable prices for raw material. If a job requires, say, fifty tons of stone, we may spend $2,000 on material before any other costs—in time, machinery, transport, or construction—are incurred. When those costs are added on, the price of the completed wall will more than double, and frequently triple or quadruple, depending on the combination of factors cited above. Fifty tons of stone will build a little more than one hundred feet of freestanding wall two feet wide and three feet high. The same amount of palletized stone delivered to the site by our local supplier, at perhaps $300 per ton, would cost our customer $14,400 before a single stone was laid.

On smaller projects, however, the difference in cost is a little less painful, and sometimes the convenience of commercially provided material is the most sensible choice. If you want to build with non-native stone, of course, there's no choice at all. But there is one important trick that can save you a lot of money and aggravation.

In many larger walls, particularly retainers, half to three-quarters of the component stones are invisible in the finished piece. That means there's no reason to build the entire wall with the weathered beauties hiding in the woods or with stones expensively packaged by suppliers. Sand and gravel yards that offer crushed stone will deliver loads of broken granite, or *riprap*, in a variety of dimensions, and this material is ideal for assembly as backing or interior bulk in larger projects. Its jagged, random shapes can be fitted into a solid mass, and its rough surface grips without sliding. It is also cheap: $8 to $12 a ton. We buy the eight-inch size, saving ourselves considerable trouble (and our customers considerable expense) by constructing the visible face and its immediate backing with "old" material, and the hidden mass with fresh chunks of smashed granite.

Even so, acquiring stone is an ongoing concern for the Owen builders. We often spend as much time getting stone to a job as we do actually building. Because we regularly use quantities of as much as one hundred tons or better, more often than not we pick and haul our own stone. We use a one-ton dump truck (which carries about three tons of stone) most of the time, but when the project is very large, we hire a ten-wheeler, which has a capacity of fifteen or more tons. The one-ton's capacity may seem stingy, but a smaller vehicle can get into places out in the woods that larger trucks cannot reach. We pick by hand into a front-end loader to avoid excessive gouging of the stones, and the unwanted dirt and debris that backhoes and excavators inevitably include, then deposit the load as carefully as possible into our truck. Some surface scarring is unavoidable, but most superficial whacks and dings color over and fade relatively quickly once the stone is settled in its new wall.

At the site we try to collect as much stone as possible before beginning to build. Sometimes there isn't the space to stockpile what we think the entire project will need, so we alternate between building and hauling. We do not sort out the stone by type, although some builders do. Over the years we've come to regard sorting as a waste of time: Sooner or later, we will use, or at least handle, almost all of the stone, anyway, and sorting out the flattest, largest, or most outstanding face stones only encourages us to use them up too soon. By simply mowing our way right through the unsorted pile, we mix the good, the bad, and the ugly all together in the project and can also look forward to the small jolts of encouragement that come from finding excellent *builders* hidden away at the bottom of the pile, just when we need them the most.

Preparation of the site itself usually involves some sort of excavation. Common sense suggests that level ground is easier to work on, and since gravity pulls stone walls straight down, a flat bearing surface offers the most effective support. Some locations require little more than a superficial scraping to make them ready. Other sites need extensive work, particularly if the project is a retaining wall. These structures should be built as if they were dams; thick at the base and tapering as they rise. A retaining wall that holds back a five-foot bank should be at least three feet thick on the bottom, *battered* (slanted) on the inside to its 12- to 18-inch-thick top. This is a method that seems nearly to have disappeared from contemporary practice, but it is very effective and in older work sometimes spectacularly thorough. We once restored an eighteenth-century house foundation whose eight-foot-tall dry stone walls were backed up at their base by more than twelve feet of carefully laid rubble.

The technique of building retaining walls as right triangles with the hypotenuse facing the uphill side guarantees that the wall will offer maximum resistance to pressure at the point where maximum pressure is exerted. This is particularly important where the fill behind the wall is new and therefore subject to heavy settling. In preparing the site for a retaining wall, you should excavate back from the planned outside face of the finished wall *at least* two-thirds of the wall's height to create enough room to lay a proper base. Dry stone retainers built with equal thickness at bottom and top, as though they were freestanding structures, are vulnerable to outward tilting and eventual collapse, as even the mildest accumulating pressure from the settling soil behind will encounter nothing substantial enough to hold it back.

Should you dig a trench or not? Conventional wisdom has it that stone walls will not last unless they stand on a footing of crushed granite or other stony material. The reason is generally given that expanding frost will heave and distort an unsupported wall, throwing it out of

RETAINER UNDER CONSTRUCTION

This cutaway drawing of a large retaining wall shows the wide footprint and the battered interior construction that gives the wall enough weight and mass to hold its bank in place. The empty space between the wall's backside and the bank will be filled with gravel and loam, and graded slightly down to the wall's cap.

line and toppling sections within a few years, if not in the wall's first winter. This is undoubtedly true in regions where winter temperatures settle in well below zero for extended periods and where ground frost penetrates a foot or more into the soil. But in many places where stone walls are common, frost seldom strikes that deep. In our own central New Hampshire area, for instance, ordinary winters do not create massive frost heaving except under exposed pavement, where very little of it is enough to push up all kinds of troublesome humps and bumps. The reputation of frost as a destroyer of stone walls, in central and southern New England anyway, is overstated. If its effects were anywhere near as devastating as advertised, the miles of untrenched antique walls we see wandering all over our countryside would not be standing after twenty years, let alone after a couple of centuries. Furthermore, a well-laid dry stone wall is a flexible structure: Most of the time, ripples and lifts instigated by frost will resettle themselves in their former positions when the ground thaws.

Of course, damaging frost heaves do occur now and then, but stone walls have a more significant enemy—their own weight. Compression of soft material under new walls as they settle is responsible for much more damage than are the freeze-thaw cycles of the winter. And it is that inevitable compression, more than the threat of frost, that makes *trenching* necessary in some cases.

What cases? That depends on where you're building. When we start a new project, we test the ground by digging a hole. If it's easy to dig with a spade alone—deep loam, loose gravel, or worst of all, sand—

we trench. If the soil is packed hard, full of stones or clay till, or impossible to excavate without a pick or a bar, we simply skim off the turf if there is any. Sometimes we just lay out our line and go, particularly when restoring or rebuilding existing work. On sites where old walls have stood for many years, the ground is precompressed and just as stable as any trench can make it.

When we do create a footing, or trench, we dig to a depth of eighteen or so inches, perhaps two feet if the underlying material is pure sand or very wet, soft soil. Our preferred fill is another form of crushed granite, one to two inches in average size. You can fill your trench with any available stone, really, but the larger the pieces, the more carefully you'll have to fit them. In his book *Stone Work*, John Jerome writes amusingly of the tedious interment of large fieldstones in the base of a wall he built and of his dismay at having to fit each one into its own reverse-impression hole. Unless that kind of punishment is one of your ancillary goals in wall building, dig yourself a nice, neat trench and get the local sand-and-gravel company to bring you a load of Crushed.

It's a good idea to dig your trench a few inches wider than the wall itself will be, particularly if it is a double-faced freestanding one. Then the critical areas under the outside edges, where compression does its worst damage, will be as stable as possible. Under retaining walls, the trench should be at least half as wide as the wall is high, but it's not necessary to trench the entire *footprint*, the area of its base, if, say, the project is an eight-foot-tall retainer with six feet of thickness at the bottom. Three or four feet, from the face in, will do. Crushed stone as fill offers the additional advantage of being rakeable, which means that smoothing it flat to receive the base stones is relatively easy. Finally, this material allows you to bed your first layer of stones tightly and firmly—twisting and gently wrenching them to and fro in place will seat them as solidly as possible, right down into the riprap.

Trenching does not prevent compression entirely, but it does slow down the process. More important, a good base equalizes settling along the entire length of the wall, so that critical base stones are much less likely to sink unevenly or otherwise squeeze themselves out of place. Stone-filled trenches also act as drains for excess water, helping to move it out from under the stones at the bottom of the wall and minimizing threats of freezing or erosion.

Whether you trench or not, you should begin by building on a level surface, particularly from front to back. Building on even a slight outward slope will invite your finished wall to slide downhill over time, an invitation it will accept with disappointing enthusiasm. Under many retaining walls, however, you can take advantage of this tendency by allowing the grade to drop a little from front to back. Downhill settlement under this circumstance will help to jam the wall against its bank even more securely without permitting enough movement to distort or unsettle the face. The fat mass of a retainer at its base generally guarantees a certain stability, but in cases where you are prevented from excavating as wide an area as you would like, the trick of in-sloping the grade can be helpful.

When the wall's footprint is cleared and leveled, you are ready to lay out a line. If the wall is straight, a simple string between stakes, about six inches off the ground, will suffice. If the wall makes angled changes of direction, drive a new stake at each break. If it curves, a garden hose or other flexible continuous marker can be laid directly on the ground and arranged in the shape you want. This line, whatever form it takes, is necessary only for the placement of the bottom *course* of stones (a "course," in mason's talk, is a horizontal row)—once that is in place, you can remove it. As you lay out the first face stones, leave a small space, an eighth of an inch or so, between the stones and the line. If you let them touch it, you run the risk of pushing the line out of place and creating a bulge that will migrate upward with each succeeding course.

Many builders string a series of lines as they go, raising their reference point along with the wall. In his *Irish Stone Walls*, master stonemason Patrick McAfee describes the use of profiles, wooden frames sized to the finished height and width of the projected wall, and set at its end points, where they can be *plumbed* and fixed in place. Lines running the length of the wall can then be attached to the profiles on both sides and raised right along with the project. This is a very precise way of maintaining horizontal and vertical dimensions, as well as the plumb, of the entire wall. For those who don't mind a little less accuracy, grade stakes at the corners will do.

While we nearly always run a line (heavy white twine works best) between stakes for our initial layout of base stones, over the years we have relied more and more on eyes alone after the first course, partly because the string gets in the way and partly because we have found that slight— *slight*—variations in the face-plane of a wall contribute something to its personality, as long as they occur within certain acceptable parameters and are not structurally inadequate. Without being disingenuous about it, a New England wall seems to look best when it's not too perfect. As we approach the top, however, we run a second string, right above the middle of the cap (the final layer of stone that tops off the wall), to give us a finishing height to shoot for.

The laying out of base stones sets a structural and aesthetic tone for the entire project. Some builders insist on a base course of the largest available stones, and while this is a sound practice from the standpoint of solidity, it does not always serve the purposes of a design scheme that seeks to show a mix of sizes throughout the wall. Our method allows the use of smaller-*looking* stones as well as large, blocky behemoths, as long as the smaller ones are not too shallow and extend back under the interior mass far enough (sixteen to twenty or more inches) to be immovably trapped. The pressure on their inside ends thus discourages

LAYOUT OF A DOUBLE-FACE
The initial stages of laying out a double-faced wall on a bed of riprap. More than half of the base stones extend well under what will become the mass of wall above them, and all are placed so that subsequent courses will have stable surfaces on which to rest.

them from canting outward as the wall settles and slipping the stones above them out of place. Because the face stones have nothing on their exposed side to keep them from falling or being pushed out, special care must be taken to ensure that their other sides are locked into the surrounding stone as tightly as possible. This is particularly critical for base stones, which must carry the greatest pressure both from above and behind, and are therefore most likely to shift or be expelled as the whole wall settles downward over time.

Base stones should be laid solidly on the ground, on their broadest, flattest sides, to offer the greatest possible resistance to the wall's relentless effort to drive them down. As you arrange them side by side, try to select stones that fit next to one another as snugly as possible, so that gaps between them, both in the face and laterally down their lengths, will be small. Base stones do not need to be of uniform height. If one that rises seven inches off the ground sits next to another that is seventeen inches high, you can make up the difference with the first stones of your second course, and proceed from there.

When your gathering, excavation, and initial layout are complete, or reasonably well established, you are ready to begin the primary activity of wall building, the practice of placement. Perhaps, however, before we get too far ahead of ourselves, now is a good time for a few words about tools, safety, and common sense.

The great—possibly the only—convenience of building dry stone walls is how little they require in the way of tools. A spade, an iron bar, and a 3-pound hammer are all you really need, and if the stones don't run much over 150 pounds or so, even the bar is optional. Builders who find it helpful to split some of their larger stones into more manageable sizes may want to use a cold chisel now and then (although the hammer alone will often suffice for this), and a steel rake comes in handy for smoothing out beds of crushed stone or gravel. Every so often, a stubborn excavation calls for a pick or a mattock. But that's about all— as Vermont poet-builder Bob Arnold puts it, "the essential tools for stonework are your two hands."

Arnold likes to celebrate the tactile sensations of ordinary country-work, so he would probably appreciate that, except on days when it's too cold, we don't wear gloves to lay stone. This may strike some beginners as masochistically eccentric, but we've found that naked hands can grip stones more securely and that it's easier to be sure where your fingers are when they're ungloved. This is an important consideration for anyone who spends substantial time setting down hard, heavy weights on places she cannot see, and for those who wish, as we do, to avoid too many repetitions of what my brother Chris long ago named *the granite kiss*, any small advantage is desirable. Disdain for gloves comes at a price, however: We endure a regular variety of small scrapes and cuts, and some types of stone, like the larger sizes of riprap we often use, are coated with a fine, abrasive dust that sands down the skin of fingertips until nerve endings begin to complain.

Serious injury, however, is not an overriding threat in stone walling, as long as builders combine patience and common sense in their approach. Always bend your knees when you lift; your legs should be tired at the day's end, not your back. Don't twist abruptly at the waist when you're straightening up with a heavy load. Make sure before you heft a large stone that it is sound. (I advise this because I once smashed myself in the mouth with the jagged end of a large, rotten stone that disengaged itself the moment I carelessly heaved away at it.) Don't throw stones around when you're working with others. (I advise *this* in memory of the time I clipped my brother in the side of the head when we were loading one day, a blow that he has either forgiven out of the goodness of his heart or forgotten due to trauma-induced amnesia.) Get some safety glasses if you're going to break or split stones with a hammer. Watch where you put your feet—tripping and falling cause more accidents on the job than anything else.

Perhaps most important, don't try to lift anything you don't have to. Stones can be rolled up planks (the Sisyphus technique, except with success), set from bucket loaders, hoisted with chains or straps, and even pried, inch by inch with a fulcrum and a bar, to move them from one place to another. You can drag stones on sleds behind tractors, push them in carts and wheelbarrows, and even create rolling conveyors for them, using short lengths of iron pipe sandwiched between two planks: The stone to be moved rests on the top plank, and the bottom plank acts as a road—just remember to keep rotating the lengths of pipe forward as the stone-carrying top plank passes each pipe by. Above all, the handling of heavy stones should be an exercise in patience. "If you can move it an inch, you can move it a mile," says Derek. The important thing is to take the time.

INCOMPLETE DOUBLE-FACE SHOWING THRUFTERS

This incomplete double-faced wall is studded with numerous thrufters of varied shapes, laid so their inside ends will pass one another in spots where the wall's width does not permit them to lie back-to-back. The carefully placed interior packing is composed of smaller junk stone, not pebbles or gravel, and is laid up to the level of the face stones—never higher—as each course is put in place.

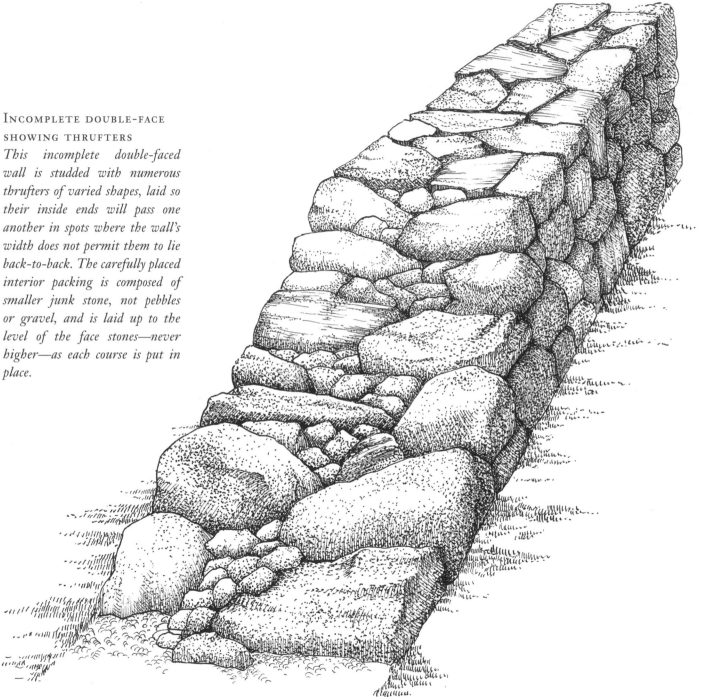

3

PLACEMENT

FITTING STONES TOGETHER

To build a stone wall, some skill is required . . . As it is a work that will last a century, it is worth doing well.
— GEORGE A. MARTIN, *Fences, Gates and Bridges* (1887)

. . . New England rounded granite is a real challenge.
— CHARLES McRAVEN, *Building with Stone* (1989)

PLACEMENT IS TO wall building as brushwork is to painting, or stitchery to a quilt. Its mastery is the single most critical requirement for both structural and artistic success in any wall. Learning to place correctly is not so much about handling material, however, as it is about learning to see, for your ongoing assessments of individual stones and the spaces you create to receive them will guide each placement you make, and eventually determine the form and texture of your project. Placement is traditionally governed by a tiny number of ancient, fundamental rules—writer John Jerome says there's only one—but they are subject to refinements that multiply exponentially as you gain experience.

The oldest and simplest rule in stone wall building is this: Put one stone on two, and two on one. More directly, this means that you should always try to place your next stone over the joint between the two (or more) below. This technique builds your wall in staggered courses, so that each stone rests on several others, two at minimum, and so that you are not constructing columns of single stones laid directly on top of one another. This is called *stack bonding*, a mistake as unsightly as it is unsound. Stack bonding produces what masons call *vertical-running joints*, cracks that travel in visibly unbroken lines through several courses. A dry wall is a unified mass, and the alternating weave of its individual members is the reason it holds itself together. Stack bonding separates the wall into structurally segregated units, reducing the dynamic interdependence of the mass and making it more apt to dis-integrate over time.

Two-on-one and one-on-two is the prime directive of dry wall construction, but it is also misleadingly incomplete, particularly for New England builders. The rule implies, for instance, that all stones are of essentially equal thickness, a patent untruth across most of our region. Beginning wallers often find that the rule's technical helpfulness ceases the moment they lay a four-inch-thick stone next to one that is ten inches thick and realize that the disparity makes it impossible to break the joint between the two with just one stone. Six inches of compensation will be required to create a stable platform for the stone in the course to come, yet the six-inch stone shouldn't be exactly as wide as the four-inch one below it, because that will produce a *stack-bond*. Two-on-one also implies that every stone laid will graciously present a nice, flat upper surface for the support of its brethren, a tragicomic assumption to anyone who has spent more than a few minutes staring at the riotous mixture of plates, blocks, triangles, ovals, trapezoids, and lumpen composites that constitute a typical supply of random field-stone. Welcome to the world of New England wall building, where "simple" rules spin off into permutations as multifarious as the shapes of the stones themselves, and few technical precepts are entirely self-explanatory.

In practice, therefore, the rule has many variations. Some builders favor larger spreads, like one on three, or five, and so on. Susan Allport met a builder who swore that one on *nine* was his personal standard, but that seems to take thoroughness into the realm of the unworkable. As a matter of practicality, you are likely to find that some of your placements are on two others, and some are on six, or four, or even (occasionally) nine. Moreover, while some of the stones you place will center themselves over the joint below with encouraging ease, others will prefer to be offset to one side or another, to cover two or more joints instead of only one, or even to settle themselves partially between the supporting stones in cases where the "joint" is actually a crevice. Precisely how the joints are broken is unimportant—what matters is that you master the trick of staggering your courses. This critical principle applies not only to the two dimensions of the visible face, but also to the interior mass of stone behind it. That's one reason *thrufters* are such precious commodities.

A thrufter is a stone with two essential attributes. It has a presentable face and a significant amount of depth, twenty-four or more inches, that will anchor it in the surrounding mass of the wall, thus providing a kind of spike to keep itself and the exposed face stones in its vicinity from squeezing out or peeling away. Thrufters extend the principle of two-on-one to the third dimension, the wall's depth, continually breaking the hidden joint between the face and its mass of backing. Though they can be long and skinny, flat and platelike, or huge and blockish, true thrufters are not numerous in an average run of New England fieldstone. They should be identified and husbanded, sought for in circumstances when they are too scarce, and spaced as evenly as possible throughout the wall. Without enough of them, say every two square feet or so, the longevity of your project will be compromised. *Thrufter*, by the way, is a word coined by Derek, perhaps from a tongue-in-cheek misreading of *thruster* in an eighteenth-century treatise on wall building, a document old enough to feature the interior cursive S that looks like an F.

The thrufter may be a New England wall builder's best friend, because the high percentage of uncooperative shapes in most supplies of random fieldstone forces the use of so much inherently unstable material. Each properly placed thrufter in a wall offers structural protection to all the stones over, under, and beside it, creating a small zone of stability around itself in which stones of inferior quality can find refuge. Grouping lesser builders and excessively spherical or misshapen backers around thrufters, then, is the best way to guarantee efficient use of your stone supply. The utility of these paragons manifests itself even before they are placed, however, for in addition to their structural value, thrufters also function as bellwethers in the flock of unlaid stones at your feet, signaling by their disappearance that it is time to refresh the supply. Notwithstanding the Yankee aphorism "use it up, wear it out, make it do, or do without," it is often a mistake to try and lay every single stone you have on hand before you haul in more. Certain kinds of projects (such as large retainers in which most of the wall's volume is hidden) will allow you to lay every stone, but in finer, smaller, or

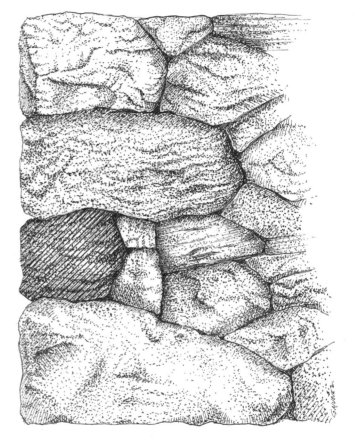

TRAPPED FACE STONE IN
CUTAWAY OF FACE
A shallow face stone is trapped between thrufters placed below and above it. The top thrufter hooks over the trapped stone slightly, helping to lock it into the wall's face. Trapping can also be done from the sides.

double-faced work, the result of such misapplied thrift will be a frustrating and increasing loss of quality, as the absence of thrufters leaves you with nothing but baseballs, canteloupes, Volkswagens, and junk. Rather than struggle for hours with no hope of success, adopt this simple guideline: No matter how much material remains to be laid, when you're out of thrufters, you're out of stone.

How do you learn to know where, exactly where, to place a

stone? "Suffice it to say," notes writer John Vivian, "that round stone and rubble wall building takes a sort of sixth sense to tell which stone goes where and in what position. Only experience can teach that."

The maddening subjectivity of any builder's personal code of placement makes instructive description difficult for teachers and pupils alike. Experience does not teach the same preferences to everyone. Still, at least two explicit, and indisputable, things can be said about placement's fundamental purpose. First, a well-placed stone lies securely in its spot, supported by stones below and beside it in a way that prevents it from rocking or slipping to the touch. Second, its positioning offers the same kind of security to stones yet to come. Keeping both these requirements in mind with every stone you lay takes some time, particularly when you're in the grip of impatience, or the stone supply isn't what it could be. John Vivian correctly points out that time and practice will refine your approach in ways no manual can teach, but as you begin, the following basic procedural guidelines will help you to make the most of your experience:

- Choose a section of some length to work on rather than a single spot. By working in an area of eight to ten feet or so, you'll give yourself multiple possibilities for placement of the stones at hand, reducing frustration and increasing efficiency as well as the quality of your placements. Ambitious traditionalists can increase their working area to 16½ feet (called a *rod* or a *perch*) and know that they

are operating with the most time-honored method of calculating the lengths of American stone walls.

- Create an even mix of the stone sizes you have on hand. This ensures that your finished face will show a consistent texture from bottom to top and end to end. Resist the impulse to lay up all your largest stones right away; this will create a steady declension in the visible dimensions of face stones as the wall rises, as well as corresponding inconsistencies in the joint patterns between stones. Stratifying walls by stone size also results in a loss of stability at the upper levels of the project, with fewer thrufters and binding *through-stones* (thrufters that are as long as the wall is wide,

SECTION OF LOW FACE SHOWING COMPENSATION FOR UNEVEN BASE STONES
The face of this low garden wall shows care in placement and an effort to mix the sizes of stones relatively evenly. Between the two largest base stones (just to the left of the center and near the right side), four smaller stones bring the wall's first lift to relative level, making it possible to lay some of the subsequent stones with their flat sides parallel to the wall's baseline. This technique gives the wall a settled, stable appearance.

showing faces on both ends) to hold the mass of smaller material together.

Sizes should be mixed within the wall as well. Since larger stones are generally more stable, it is a mistake to deprive a wall's internal core of their steadying influence. Walls filled indiscriminately with small pebble-ish waste stone are asking for trouble—these stones will tend to stretch and spread their outer containment the way marbles stretch and flatten a leather bag when it is dropped, because their small sizes enable them to slip and settle too easily amongst one another. Their movement builds up undue pressure at the base of the wall that can only escape by pushing face stones out, or by prying larger builders apart. Careful use of large and small stones throughout the wall's core helps minimize this tendency.

• Test your placements by adjustment and experimentation. Especially when you are beginning, make certain to explore each stone's full range of possibilities, turning, flipping, and re-laying it every possible way before you assign it to a spot for good. Sometimes a stone will glide perfectly into position with an almost clairvoyant click, settling itself as if by instinct the moment you first lay it down. Many more times, you'll have to make adjustments, but the stones will often discover better perches than your eyes can find, as long as you give them a chance to do so. Roll them over, turn them around, try showing different faces, or even laying them in different spots, if you (or they) aren't satisfied with how they sit or how they look.

Finally, don't hesitate to discard or set aside stones that simply refuse to cooperate. This practice is every bit as important with backers as it is with face stones, not only because it produces superior placement and tighter fitting in general, but because it allows the stones themselves to become your instructors. Turning and flipping may seem to slow your progress in the short term, but will actually accelerate your overall development as a builder, improving your vision as well as your tactile familiarity with the stones.

- *Back up* everything as you go. This is one of the hardest habits to acquire but perhaps the most useful. In retaining walls, for every face stone or group of face stones that you lay, the next step is to build up the interior of the wall directly behind them, to, but not above, the high point of the face row. Avoid stacking two or more layers of face stone without backing up, no matter how tempted you may be to do so. By filling behind each face stone all the way to the back of the section, you prepare the wall immediately to receive its next course of faces, and you steadily use up the supply of faceless rubble in your pile. In double-faced walls, work your section back and forth from one face to the other so that neither side gets too much higher at any given time. This process is a little fussier, but it helps to maintain the wall's integrity by allowing you to weave alternating thrufters from each side, course by course, as you go up. In double-faced walls thirty or less inches wide, you'll find that thrufters often cannot lie tail-to-tail on opposite sides—they have to pass each other alternately, so that the stone in the face opposite a given thrufter is often fairly shallow. Bringing both sides up simultaneously allows you to trap these shallower stones more effectively than you might by building only one side at a time. Narrow double-faced walls allow the use of through-stones as well, which, though exceptionally stabilizing, are usually not very plentiful.

- Teach yourself to trap—then avoid doing it. *Trapping* is a technique that compensates for a weakness in placement by positioning a stone so that it cannot escape the wall, even if the stone is shallow or poorly shaped. It can be done in two ways. The first is to position the wider, fatter, or bulkier end of the stone inside the wall, and the narrower or pointed end in the face. This technique is used to line dry stone wells, and it is extremely effective because it locks a stone inside the mass. The only drawback to this method is that it often requires you to show a face that is not particularly flat, hardly a face at all. Be careful that you aren't leaving an inconsistent dimple or protrusion that will draw the eye. The second trapping technique, useful when you can't avoid laying a very shallow face stone, is to anchor it from above or at its sides with a much larger stone (or stones). If carefully placed, this larger stone will not only clamp the lower, smaller one into position, but it will also distribute pressure away from the smaller stone, helping to avoid later problems. A general note: Trapping should not be a first choice in

most situations. It's rarely as effective, either artistically or structurally, as sound basic placement.

- *Place* every stone. Developing this habit calls for a little self-
discipline. Many beginning builders spend disproportionate care on
face stones and pay much less attention to the wall's interior
structure, hurriedly dropping or even tossing their *backers* into position so that they can get on with the next course of facing material.
This would be a perfectly adequate approach if stones were helpful and proactive creatures with a desire to assist impatient wall
builders. But stones do not desire to assist. They desire to rest, as
completely and stably as possible, and in a dry stone wall they
will migrate ceaselessly, if slowly, from one resting place to another
until they encounter resistance that stops them for good. The
unstable fits and consequent gaps created by careless internal
placements allow stones the freedom to follow their anarchic bliss
and open the way to eventual interior collapse. As the center of
a badly filled wall reorders and compresses itself, it sinks down.
Upper sections of the wall's face are then gradually deprived of
their supporting mass of backers, and they sag inward, while
increasing pressure ratchets up behind the face stones at or near the
base of the wall. These stones may then begin to work their way out
of the face and sooner or later release themselves, causing what we
call a *blowout*.

  Internal collapse is a primary cause of problems in larger dry stone structures, and it is the reason a great many of our wide antique walls, which once stood straight, now appear to be battered, with uneven, spreading bases and sides that lean inward to a sunken cap. We can forgive the old farmer-builders for carelessness in their construction: They were largely unconcerned with anything but disposal of ton upon ton of plow-shattering field rubble and so threw up great causeways of stone specifically as running dumpsters for the annual crop of "New England potatoes" they turned up in the spring. No one can blame them for throwing stones into their walls, but we no longer have their good excuse. Place every stone.

- Lay both face stones and internal backing stones on the level, whenever possible. This dictum is subject to dispute among experienced wall builders, who in some cases advocate laying outside face stones on a slight inwardly inclined plane to keep them from slipping or being pushed out of the face later on. In many walls this technique works perfectly well, but there are two drawbacks. One is that stones will tend to accept any invitation to slide, in any direction. Installation on a slope encourages them to shift their positions relative to one another as the mass of the wall settles, increasing the potential for distortion and instability. Second, stones laid sloping inward will reflect that slope in the visible angles of their faces, which will tip back into the wall's face from bottom to top instead of presenting true vertical planes. This is acceptable in a wall with a relatively rough or battered face, but in work meant to be tightly fitted and straight up and down, such leaning faces give a ramshackle appearance, even if their placements are sound.

How can you know what "level" is when the stones you're working with are largely rounded, ovate, or randomly polygonal? In these instances, simply determine the stone's center of gravity, and place that center as near as can be to the low side. One way of identifying a very round stone's center is to roll it back and forth on the ground a little until it comes to rest on its own. Another is to pick it up and observe the position in which it rests most comfortably in your grip. It's usually easier to heft a stone, particularly a heavy one, when its center of gravity is down. Top-heaviness makes the stone harder to manage in your hands, and this is precisely the instability you will build into the wall if too many of its members are laid at dependent, sloping angles.

Of course, you'll find it all but impossible to make every single placement a dead-level one. But the more you do, the more stable your wall will be, for a very simple reason. Every stone laid at dead level is being pulled straight down, and straight down only. It is not shunting off to one side or another or leaning and pushing against neighboring stones, except the ones directly below. The shifts, settlings, and collective adjustments that all dry walls make over time are far less likely to result in problems if the majority of individual placements enlist gravity as an ally rather than antagonize its infi-

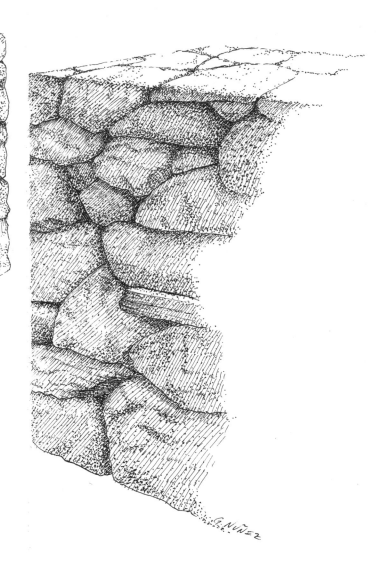

CUTAWAY SHOWING INTERIOR CHINKING

This cutaway of a double-faced wall shows how interior chinking helps level the placement of face stones. The three heavily shaded stones in the exposed end provide stable surfaces for the stones above them.

nite, implacable patience. Level laying, then, is a major contributor to the longevity of your wall.

- Chinking. *Chinking* is the practice of stuffing or jamming small chips or fragments of stone between larger builders to stabilize them or to fill too-large cracks in a wall's face. In certain types of construction, such as walls or foundations made of very large, roughly quarried blocks or slabs that cannot be tightly fitted as they are, chinking is as necessary as it is effective. Many builders commonly use the method in all kinds of projects, with all types of stone.

  We discourage chinking, however. For one thing, correct placement alone should seat a stone solidly, without requiring the adjustment provided by a *chinker.* Since chinking allows the use of certain stones in certain spots that more scrupulous attention to placement would avoid, the technique quickly becomes a habit that encourages sloppy or careless building. Furthermore, chinkers themselves are among the least stable stones in a wall: too small to resist movement by virtue of their own weight or mass, and disconnected from the interwoven integrity of the wall as a whole, they are the first stones to be dislodged or squeezed out of place when the wall begins to settle and shift. If too many of the larger structural stones depend on chinkers, their eventual loss produces significant weakening throughout the mass, and when chinkers are overused in the face of a wall, as filler for gaps and cracks, they visibly betray the builder's inattention to proper fitting.

Like trapping, however, chinking can be helpful if practiced moderately. The technique is most effective when used under the backsides or ends of face stones to level them off for the next course. (Patrick McAfee calls such interior chinkers spalls, a terrific word.) Chinkers placed from behind can themselves be backed up with other stones in the wall's interior, giving them at least a reasonable chance of staying put. In our excavations of old stonework, we have noted time and again how little reliance the old-timers placed on chinking, either cosmetically or structurally. With a few exceptions, such as those noted above, the method was evidently not a reliable one for them.

"Stones are like people—some are good to work with. They fit in anywhere, but others are cranky. You've got to humor them. Leave them to one side a bit and you'll find a place for them all right." This cogent bit of analysis is attributed to a man named Tom Newing, who built stone walls for fifty years in New South Wales, Australia. Newing died in 1927, but his words capture perfectly the patience, and the persistence, that are critical to thoughtful and effective placement. Stones *are* like people, with individual personalities that express themselves as shapes, and the builder's job, in a way, is to surround each one with a group of compatible partners that conform to one another, nest on, over, and against one another, and compensate for one another's weaknesses as readily and familiarly as possible. The quality of the harmony among shapes that you build into your wall, stone by stone, is directly responsible for its beauty and a major contributor to its longevity.

Placement is the heart of wall building, its essential activity, and a source of deep satisfaction when it is going smoothly. Many beginning builders experience something like a sense of triumph in the act of setting a stone in a spot that's just right, and this feeling matures but does not fade, even after years of practice. "I never tire of the game of fitting stones together," says Charles McRaven, hinting with his use of the word *game* at an attitude of grave playfulness that seems to take hold of the imagination of many wall builders. Mastery of placement gives more than just pleasure, however, for it also teaches a complex and personal appreciation for shape, form, and pattern. No one who learns to build ever looks at a stone wall quite the same way again, and to eyes instructed by the practice of placement, no two walls are ever quite alike.

STEPS WITH LANDINGS AND DIRECTION-CHANGE
IN CORNER OF RETAINER

This set of steps takes the place of a standard corner at the convergence of per-
pendicular retaining walls. The left side corner is the beginning of a return,
and the right side becomes a freestanding butt end. The steps change direction
and feature very deep treads. The surface stones of the landings, behind the
leading edges of each tread, are laid onto a carefully placed and compacted bed
of gravel over riprap, as though they were in a walkway or a patio.

FACES

4

STONES THAT SHOW AND THE CREATION OF SURFACES

I never yet beheld that special face
Which I could fancy more than any other.

— SHAKESPEARE, *The Taming of the Shrew*

IN STONE WORK, the word *face* has two meanings. It can refer to that part of an individual stone that is visible in a finished wall, or to the outside surface of the wall as a whole. Faces are what shows; the parts of the wall, and of each stone in it, that you can see when the wall is complete. Like the pieces of a puzzle or the tiles in a mosaic, the individual stones in any wall unite to produce a visual plane with particular characteristics of texture and shape. When the elements of that plane are presented in a balanced and harmonious pattern, our eyes are drawn where they should be, to the presence of the wall's entirety in the landscape rather than to any particular part of it.

That is why consistency is so critical in the matter of choosing the individual "faces" you present as you build. A wall that groups many large rounded stones together in one section, for instance, while a nearby segment of small, squarish, or broken dinner plates offers a very different look, or one that features enormous boulders all the way along its base but upper courses composed of much smaller stones or a scattered topping of tiny pebbles, will always look off-balance somehow and cannot settle into its surroundings with the satisfying architectural comfort that makes a good wall such a pleasure to see. But this does not mean that you have to seek out a large supply of identical stones to create a proper wall. The vast differences in color, shape, and texture among individuals in an average run of New England fieldstones can be used to great advantage, as long as they are blended in a consistent mix throughout the overall face.

The flatter the individual faces you present, the smoother and finer your wall will look. But absolutely flat faces are by no means a prerequisite for handsomeness in a New England stone wall. Admirable work can be done with stones that offer very little in the way of sheared or neatly flattened sides or ends, as long as you pay attention to the amount of depth you allow the face of the wall to occupy. This means making a decision about the degree of roughness you desire or are willing to tolerate in the finished product.

Think of the face of a wall as a plane, an imaginary vertical surface against which the wall's outside stones are laid. Your strings mark the position of this surface as you construct the wall. Most of the time we think of the strings and their implied plane as a two-dimensional guide, indicating only the horizontal and vertical positioning of the wall's projected face. But it is possible to imagine a second plane, parallel to the first and set somewhere to the inside of it. The space between these two planes is a kind of window, an even, theoretical distance of any depth you choose. Let's say six inches.

If you think of the face of your wall as a single two-dimensional plane, you must lay your face stones right up against it as closely as possible to create a correspondingly flat-faced wall. The surfaces of individual face stones and the joints between them must meet this plane or come very close to it, and only the flattest faces will allow that kind of precision. But if you think of the wall's face as a window, a six-inch-deep space, then individual stones and their joints have only to fall somewhere within its prescribed depth in order to conform. This results in a rougher outside surface, but it also allows a much more liberal view of what constitutes a "face" on individual stones. All of a sudden, all kinds of knobby, wracked, and rounded stones become acceptable as facing material, and your chances of having enough of them to complete the project are mightily increased. As long as the most extreme projection point of a face stone (Ian Cramb calls it the *snout*) does not break the outside plane, and the joints between stones are not set farther back than the inside plane, your wall will show a consistency of depth in its overall face, and its roughness will become part of its charm. This notion of a *plane window* sounds more complex

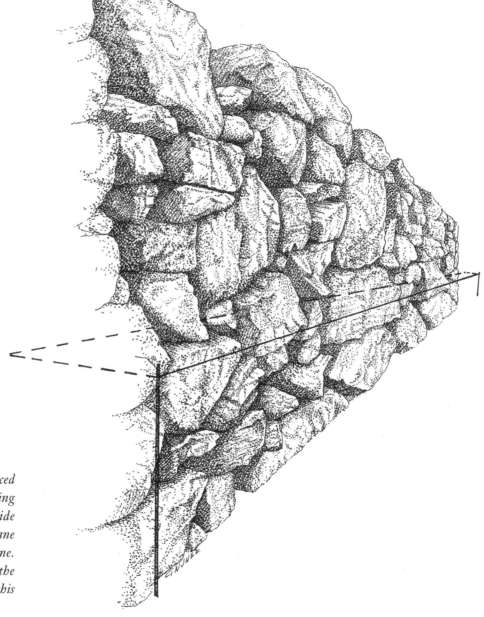

SECTION OF ROUGH FACE
SHOWING PLANE WINDOW
*A short section of rough-faced
wall with the outside guide string
still in place and the inside
boundary of an imaginary "plane
window" marked as a dotted line.
The joints and faces of all the
visible stones must fall within this
space.*

than it really is, but with New England fieldstone the maintenance of a consistent degree of roughness is essential if you want the wall to look right.

A good stonemason tries to avoid breaking rocks. See, when you fracture rocks, you get a fresh surface. You want to try to keep the weathered look to your wall . . . So the best thing to do is avoid trimming.

—WALL BUILDER HARVEY BIXBY

Many builders cut or trim individual stones, using hammers, chisels, or the old feather-and-wedge system, which requires the drilling of a series of holes along the line where you want the   split, then the careful driving of small steel spikes b   rs, slightly cupped steel spreaders abou   This is an involved process s   another will split   ys cre-
at   aying
stin   t of
large
    Bu   n
Harvey   e
of a sto
stone wal   in
waiting twe   ally. We may

use a mason's hammer or a cold chisel now and then to split thick slabs of shale into smaller plates or to remove structurally troublesome protuberances, but only in places where the new surface won't show. Most of the time we lay what we have in front of us, as is.

The notion that there exists a substance that will age the surfaces of stones in a short time has provided us with one of the most amusing running discussions we've had with wall lovers over the years. Impassioned testimony has been heard in favor of many candidates, including buttermilk, tea made from horse manure, urine of various origins, and so on. While we hesitate to summarily dismiss the claims of those who have personal experience with this sort of alchemy, we've never actually seen such recipes work. Nevertheless, given the widespread willingness to believe in such a substance, we have from time to time considered packaging a secret amalgam of nameless compounds, to be sold under the brand name Mosslgro. Somehow, we never got around to it. Perhaps the prospect of mixing it up was enough to deter us. It's easier, after all, and much less malodorous, to build our walls with face stones honestly aged.

The trick with an individual stone is to learn to recognize whether any of its sides or ends is presentable as a face. This is more than a matter of simply finding a (relatively) flat surface somewhere upon it. Single stones may have more than one face or none at all. But no face is presentable unless the stone that carries it can be soundly laid on the previous course and can soundly support the courses yet to come.

Beginning builders often find that recognizing potential faces on a stone is fairly easy, but recognizing them in combination with the right structural characteristics takes a little longer. The face of a stone may be attractive for its flatness, for moss or lichen growing on it, or for a striking pattern or color in the stone itself, but it is useless unless it can be correctly placed. This frustrating reality accounts for the phenomenon of the *cheap seducer*.

A cheap seducer is a stone that appears at first glance to be ideal for presentation as part of your wall's face. Imagine a twenty-four-inch football-shaped thrufter, for instance, with one of its end points sheared off. You may be able to make its flat end meet the plane of the wall's face or fall within its window perfectly well, but because the widest part of its girth is in the middle, the outer edges of face stones laid beside it will not meet the edges of *its* face, leaving noticeable gaps. Other cheap seducers create *ski jumps*, with upper surfaces that slope out and down, offering no support for the next course of face stones. All attempts to place a cheap seducer, then, are doomed by structural defects that prevent its stable installation on previous work or the laying of later stones upon or around it.

Cheap seducers occur in a variety of guises. They can be too round or too shallow, or angularly misshapen in any number of unhelpful ways. Once identified, they should be consigned to oblivion as backers or discarded altogether. The insistent impulse to lay them into the wall's face in spite of their defects should be resisted—this almost always results in visual or structural anomalies that cannot be corrected and that will leap out at you accusingly, forever after, as you contemplate your work.

Not every stone that causes trouble is a cheap seducer, however—a subtle fact that will become clear when you learn to appreciate the merits of the *problemsolver*. No matter how diligently you work to mate the shapes of primary builders in a consistently snug pattern, the obstinate vagaries of New England fieldstone make compromise inevitable. Many times you'll find that a particular stone sits just right in a certain spot—*except* for its wretched matchup with one other stone, usually to its right or left in the same course, which, for one reason or another, leaves an ugly, deep, and eye-catching gap in the face of the wall. (For some reason now lost in the mists of time, we call these unsightly canyons *cat caves*.) Sometimes there's no solution but to remove one or both of the offenders and begin again. But when the cave is deep enough, it is often possible to lay a long, narrow fragment into the space between the builders. This is a problemsolver, a stone that can take the shape of anything from a cigar to a miniature croquet mallet but whose defining quality is its willingness to serve as a spatial ambassador between face stones that are incompatible, filling the cat cave *and* lying deeply enough in the wall's face to be integral to its structure. Because of this, a problemsolver is not a chinker: It is laid into the face at the time of construction, not as an afterthought. The efficacy of problemsolvers is so great that any long (ten or more inches), narrow, oddly sculpted stone resembling a stick, a knife, a tent peg, or a wedge should be set aside as soon as it appears and never wasted in a wall's interior.

The visible surfaces of a wall do not consist merely of its sides and ends, but also its cap. On very rough and single-stack walls, the New England tradition does not spend a great deal of time fussing with uniformity or careful fitting in its caps, which need only be heavy enough to resist easy dislodging and arranged to show some consistency of height to give the wall a coherent line. On more finely fitted and double-faced walls, the options for capping are partly a matter of taste and partly a function of available material.

One of the advantages of battered walls is their relatively narrow tops, which make possible the installation of what we call a *hard cap*, a binding layer of thick, relatively flat stones selected and laid to cover the entire width of the wall, almost like a roof. This kind of cap helps trap the smaller stones beneath, resists disarrangement by people and animals, and even sheds a fair amount of water. Such caps can be laid on wider, unbattered walls as well, if the right stones are available, although they may have to be lined up in two or three rows instead of one. More often, especially on longer walls, a supply of heavy, flat stones sufficient to cover the entire surface of the cap is difficult to come by. In these cases we resort to the *puddle cap*, a compromise that allows the use of heavier material only on the outer edges of the wall's two sides, with a filling of smaller, less shapely stones in between.

In the British Isles and in some parts of the United States, like Kentucky, the plentiful presence of broken, flat stones of a certain size makes possible the traditional technique called *coping*, in which a single row of stones is set on edge, like a shelf of books, to finish off a wall's cap. The style is highly distinctive and has the additional virtue of raising the overall height of a wall with the least possible amount of stone, but since most of New England offers relatively small or nonexistent supplies of uniformly flat stones, the region's wall builders coped as best they could. The result is a variety of traditional strategies, from caps of large and small fieldstones to layers of split plates. Around many cemeteries and on other public or merely prominent stone walls, the practice of capping with long, quarried or split slabs of granite became widespread, particularly in the nineteenth century. Striking examples of this style survive all over New England, and it is a highly effective alternative to traditional coping, although difficult to repair once the supporting walls begin to fail. In capping, as in every other aspect of New England wall building, appearances are dictated less by unbending custom than by a practical response to circumstance and inclination.

I never tire of the game of fitting stones, none of which are even similar. Bricks, now, and concrete blocks, have that moronic sameness that makes them better building materials, but endears them to no creative person.

—CHARLES MCRAVEN, *Building with Stone*

Stone work calls for creativity in at least two ways. First, of course, is the design of the structure as a whole; its length, height, and thickness, its relationship to other features of the landscape, and the degree to which it expresses some kind of function. But as Charles McRaven implies, there is another, subtler creative dimension in the act of building, which lies in the preferences of individual builders for particular patterns in the faces of their walls. The rules of engineering in dry stone construction permit enormous variation in surface patterning, and part of learning the craft is the discovery of your own characteristic geometry, the way *you* like to see stones fit together.

Beginning builders often create inconsistent, nearly chaotic patterns in their first walls, but after a time a certain regularity will begin to emerge. This is not entirely a matter of deliberate manipulation. Conscious choices to present certain stones in certain ways can play an important part in the development of a "style," but characteristic patterns will also develop simply through the repetitive practice of sound structural principles. In other words, the individualism in your building style will largely take care of itself if you concentrate on building well and consistently. "This art of 'dry masonry' used to be so well known," said artist Eric Sloane, "that you could just look at a wall or a foundation and recognize it as the work of a particular builder."

Derek's special idiosyncrasies are the crossed T, one thin, flat stone set vertically in the face with another similar stone laid horizontally just above it, and the dotted I, a thin, flat vertical set directly below a round stone. (You can see an example of the first of these in Bill Nuñez's drawing opposite the Introduction on page XVIII—look for it just under the wall's cap, directly above the culvert opening.) Distinctive as they are, however, these humorous punctuations do not define Derek's essential style. This is considerably more difficult to describe, although it is, as Eric Sloane points out, quite recognizable. The stones in Derek's walls look comfortable. They appear to be laid in ways they might choose for themselves, if they had the choice. They are level and settled, insofar as their shapes permit, and they nest together in his best work as though habit had conformed them to one another, as though they had permitted their sides and edges to yield, just slightly, to receive the intimate press of their neighbors. Derek's walls are not spectacularly tight in the formal mason's way, but their fitting expresses a great and consistent sense of care, as though each stone had something to offer and none were unimportant. They have, if such a thing can be said about a stone wall, a kind of tenderness.

Stephanie and I learned from Derek, and so we build as he does in many essential ways. Yet our walls are less poetical. Having returned to repair enough of them over the years to develop a healthy appreciation for the occasional price of overinfatuation with our own artistry, we've arrived at an abiding commitment to structural matters. Techniques of placement that ensure the stability of each stone in the wall also, as a general rule, contribute a certain visual integrity to its face. Good walls will stand, and they will *look* like they will stand, too. We have no special signifiers, although we often present particular stones in particular spots because we take a fancy to them. The choices of facing we make tend to be dictated practically, by the stone at hand and by the immediate needs of the project. Our walls are slightly tougher looking than Derek's, a bit blockier at times, but also settled and stoical. We try to build a wall that looks as though it was already there before we started.

Whatever the idiosyncrasies of its individual style, the face of a wall is its public statement, its functional declaration, and its testimony for, or against, the skill of its maker. Stone walls contain a personal file of sorts on their builders, a record of good and bad days, degrees of laziness, commitment, experience, humor, and care. Stonework can praise you, endure you, or gossip about you. The face of the wall you build is likely to display your best personal qualities and your worst, often simultaneously, to anyone who knows how to read its language. Part of the fascination of making your own faces, then, is what it teaches you to see in the faces of walls you never touched.

RETAINER EMERGING TO
DOUBLE-FACE
A simple retaining wall for most
of its length, this construction
rises above its bank in the fore-
ground and becomes a double-
faced freestanding wall that sits
atop the continuing retainer.

5

SPECIAL STRUCTURES

VARIATIONS ON A THEME

Nothing older than stone but the soil and the sea and the sky.
Nothing stronger than stone but water and air and fire.
Nothing worthier than stone but the harpstring, the word and the tree.
Nothing humbler or stubborner than stone—whatever it be!

—ROBERT FARREN

The products of my farm are these,
Sufficient for my own

—EMILY DICKINSON

WALLS ARE FAR from the only dry stone structures New England's resourceful farmer-builders devised. Like Legos or Tinkertoys, fitted stone will conform to any number of configurations and design schemes—indeed, one of the reasons stone was employed so extensively as building material, aside from its endless availability, was its extraordinary usefulness for a variety of purposes, from single boulders set as post footings under barn floors to the most elaborate ramps, stiles, wells, and foundations. All of these constructions remain variations of the two basic types of wall, the freestanding and the retainer, although Yankee ingenuity frequently blended variations of both forms in contiguous pieces of work. This chapter discusses the characteristics and functions of some of these special structures and a few of the particular considerations of builders who undertake them. There are also some notes about certain arrangements frequently incorporated within walls themselves, such as steps, curves, corners, returns, and planters. The topics are arranged roughly in order of their degree of difficulty.

WALKS AND PATIOS

WHEN I WAS very young, long stretches of the dirt road I (still) live on became virtually impassable for a few weeks each year in the early spring, when the departure of ground frost turned the road's gravel to a bottomless river of mud. Diligent road agents with better equipment long ago put an end to Brockway Road's annual meltdown, but in an older, more rural New England, without paving or diesel graders, this temporary condition became a season unto itself, a time when roads, fields, and even footpaths seemed to dematerialize as if by some sort of malevolent, soggy magic. At the Shaker Village in Canterbury, New Hampshire, the indefatigable residents resisted at least one aspect of mud season's dreary grip by installing a network of stone walkways among most of the community's main buildings. These walkways are typical Shaker constructions; simplicity itself in design, spectacularly clean in execution. They are slabs of stone, four feet wide, in varying lengths of up to ten or twelve feet, shaped to fit one another end-to-end and meticulously lined up in arrow-straight rows. Fully laid out by the 1840s, the walkways provided mud-free passage around the village in the spring, and their smooth, dark surfaces absorbed heat from the sun, helping to melt away residual snow and ice when they were cleared in the wintertime.

The Shakers were famous for their thoroughness but also for their practicality. Although their walkway builders shaped and matched each component slab for surface consistency and end-to-end fit, they were less meticulous about the way they bedded the stones in the ground—at least by contemporary standards. These days, most walks and stone or brick patios are laid over carefully compacted layers of gravel, which provide drainage and a level surface for installation. The Shakers didn't bother with any of that, as we discovered when we took up some sections of their walkways and relaid them more than 150 years after they were first put in place. We found that their builders had simply laid the slabs in the ground, digging reverse-impression beds for each stone and propping it into place with a few small fieldstones before shoveling some of the excavated dirt back into the remaining spaces underneath. Over time the slabs had begun to heave up and down a bit, creating bumpy mismatches between individual stones that made walking an invitation to trip, and wheelchair passage a minor form of torture. There's no way of knowing exactly when the successive actions of frost, water, settling, and human traffic began to tilt the Shakers' massive walkway slabs, and it's likely that something like the same sort of misalignment would have taken place, after 150 years, even if the stones had been laid into beds of gravel. We suspect that they remained snugly in place for at least a century, a record of longevity for which the Shakers relied on mass and weight alone.

This is the old-fashioned way with walks and patios, perfectly effective as long as the stones you choose are thick and heavy enough to seat themselves irresistibly. A 150- or 200-pound stone with four or more inches of thickness is unlikely to loosen or to start to rock underfoot, particularly if it is carefully supported with packed stones and soil. Unevenness on the bottom side doesn't matter, since you can simply shape the hole to accommodate the stone. The Shaker slabs, some of which weigh well over a ton, are remarkably variable in thickness, running from two or three inches to more than a foot, sometimes on the same stone.

There are two advantages to this method: First, it is far less elaborate and invasive than conventional construction, which calls for a general excavation of the entire walk or patio area, the removal of excavated material and its partial replacement with crushed gravel, and the spreading, leveling, and compaction of that gravel before any stone can be laid down. The second advantage is flexibility, an important factor for those of us who do not have at our disposal gangs of skilled Shaker brethren to quarry, prepare, and transport large quantities of perfectly flat stone slabs. Old-fashioned stone-by-stone interment means you can install a project piecemeal, laying in single stones or small sections as you locate them, without committing yourself all at once to the labor and disruption of the whole. Removal of excavated material is easier, too; simply a matter of hauling off the dirt each stone displaces. Finally, the absence of a prepared bed eliminates any structural restrictions on shape or thickness, leaving you free to use odd or eccentric stones, or to create patterns that please you.

PLANTERS

AN INNOVATION DEVELOPED largely by contemporary wall builders, planters are usually low retaining structures filled not with gravel or waste stone but with loam, to create raised beds for flowers, shrubs, or even vegetables. Planters are particularly useful where the soil is untillable or simply poor, and they also provide excellent drainage, as their unmortared walls cannot contain excess water. (For the same reason, they also tend to dry out faster than in ground planting beds.)

Stone planters fit nicely into design schemes that incorporate other, more substantial stonework. A planter set in front of a higher retaining wall, for instance, creates a kind of two-tiered terracing effect that not only protects and contains its flower bed, but also provides it with a backdrop of fitted stone. As many gardeners know, the juxtaposition of delicate flowers with rugged stone is an intensely pleasing marriage of opposites.

There are two particular considerations to keep in mind when building a planter. First is the general challenge presented by any low or relatively small dry stone structure, which, because it does not have enough sheer mass to bind its individual stones as tightly as larger, heavier walls, tends to come apart more easily over time. This is especially true of retaining walls, which must not only hold themselves together but also resist the pressure of settling soil on their backsides. A planter, then, must be fitted with extra care, composed of the most substantial sizes its design will accept visually, and faced largely, if not entirely, with stones that run well into the mass of wall. It's also a good idea, if possible, to cap a planter wall with relatively heavy stones. These will not only help to stabilize the structure, but will also resist the human traffic of gardening and sitting that lower walls inevitably attract. If the *capstones* are also thick—five or six inches or more—so much the better. Then the area of the planter immediately behind them will have enough soil depth to support plantings right up to the stone itself. When the cap is very thin, the graduated mass of backing stone occupies most of the interior space just behind the capstones, and there isn't much room for things to grow near the planter's outer edges.

The second trick with planters is to arrange the inside slope of their walls as tightly as possible to discourage the soil they contain from washing out through the joints between stones. Make sure that any large spaces are chinked with chips or small shards, so that escape rivulets cannot develop during summer downpours. In larger retaining walls there's a certain amount of room for soil or gravel to settle in among the stones as the years go by without feeling the necessity to escape, but the lower, thinner walls of planters don't have as much of that absorbent capacity. If built too loosely, they will simply allow water and soil to spew out through the face. Tight packing on the inside will help the soil stay put until it settles in place and the root systems of plants have developed well enough to bind it further. For skeptics who require additional thoroughness, manufacturers produce various types of landscape fabric, which can be laid over the stones on the insides of planters after they have been built, and then buried when the planter is filled. This material is porous enough to let water pass through, but its mesh holds back the soil itself. The only drawback of landscape fabrics is that they can sometimes become clogged with tiny particulates that reduce or negate their ability to pass water easily, making proper drainage difficult. In most cases, carefully laid stonework will suffice. One caution bears repeating here, however: Never, ever, fill planters (or any retaining wall) with sand, unless you're anxious to study extensive sediment dispersal patterns on your lawn or driveway the morning after the next heavy rain. Aside from water itself, nothing comes pouring out of stone walls more easily.

Most planters are discrete retaining structures, but it is also possible to create them inside the caps of wide double-faced walls by removing the interior stone between the faces to a depth of a foot or eighteen inches and replacing it with soil. In existing walls, this may require rebuilding some sections of face to give them retaining capacity they do not have once their backing is removed. When you've hollowed out the cap, be sure to stuff the joints at the sides and bottom of the space thoroughly or line the trough you've created with landscape fabric.

Ramps

Because farmers needed wide access to as many levels of their barns as possible, to accommodate animals or teams drawing wagons, carts, or sleighs, they often designed these buildings with open foundations on one side or end. This allowed easy entry to the level below the building itself, but it also tended to raise one or more of the structure's upper entrances above grade. Furthermore, the hilly terrain in so much of New England meant that a great many barns (and houses) were built on slopes, a necessity that helped farmers to create access to the building's understory by exposing it naturally on the downhill side but that also elevated upper levels far from the ground. That is why so many old New England barns feature stone ramps at one or both ends, some of which reach as high as the barn's second story (see the illustration on page 20).

Ramps are nothing more than parallel retaining walls laid back-to-back, rising at a manageable grade from ground level to a building's entrance. Where they run alongside a rising slope, they can also be built as single retainers contained by stone on the downhill side and by the hill itself on the other. Ramps were often built almost entirely of stone, with a relatively thin surface of gravel or soil laid over them to smooth out the roadbeds they carried. Because they are so massive, they are also handy repositories for waste stone, functioning not just structurally, but also as storage for rubble that would otherwise have had to be hauled away.

It's curious, in a way, that New Englanders don't seem to think of building ramps anymore. They're extremely useful wherever something large, like a car or even a riding mower, must regularly travel from one level to another on a relatively gradual incline. Their utility is not confined to the approaches to buildings, either: Farmers often constructed ramps as connectors between sections of land separated by gullies, wet spots, or sudden changes in elevation, adapting the same back-to-back retaining wall design to create rough causeways or bridges, sometimes with a stone-lined culvert at the bottom to let water pass through.

FOUNDATIONS

ADMIRERS OF OLD stonework usually learn their appreciation from walls, but a great deal of the finest dry masonry still to be seen in New England is not found along forested boundary lines or between fields, but in the stone foundations of houses and barns. Even in places where the buildings have long since disappeared, the half-filled cellar holes of abandoned homesteads all over rural New England reveal a marvelous array of clever, practical designs in dry stonework executed with breathtakingly skillful craftsmanship. Whether constructed of great, sheared boulders, laid so snugly they seem to have been carved to fit, or pieced together from hundreds of thousands of smaller fieldstones, the best of the old foundations exhibit levels of care and creativity few walls can match. Here are stone-lined passageways once covered by bulkheads, descending ramps and steps, and root-cellar annexes set apart from the larger excavation. Some foundations contain enormous freestanding pillars of dry-laid stone that once supported a central chimney and its many fireplaces, and even stone-lined wells built partially into the foundation itself or dug straight down from the cellar floor. Enclosing all of this are the walls, six to eight feet tall, laid in precise rectangles or squares and very often still standing—if undisturbed by trees, water, or pilferage—as straight as the day they were laid.

Foundations, of course, are in most cases retaining walls built not only to support the building above, but to contain the earthen sides of the excavation they enclose. Many of them were capped with roughly dressed slabs of granite, a technique that helped to distribute the weight of the building relatively evenly across the stonework, as well as raising its wooden walls slightly away from the damp and damaging ground. In other cases, the long, hand-hewn sills of the house or barn were laid directly on the fitted stone, which might be allowed to emerge from its excavation to show a low outside face underneath the sill. Still others might be finished off with mortared work, in stone or even brick.

Foundation builders favored large, heavy stones unlikely to be dislodged. Where the subsoil permitted it, they built their walls thickly, particularly at the base, a technique that required the builders to excavate areas much larger than the size of the finished cellar, to accommodate all that stone. Behind the visible faces of thousands of old foundations, whether lost in the woods or still carrying their buildings, lie massive amounts of hidden rubble laid up with the angled batter that guarantees a bottom-heavy stability, and enough interlocking mass to hold itself together and settle evenly through the years. These walls are models of the proper way to construct a New England retaining wall, and though few homebuilders can manage the time or expense to build them today, dry stone foundations remain among the most artful and characteristic architectural legacies of the region. Interestingly, the basic design of dry stone foundations is similar to that of another New England stone structure, the town pound. Surviving examples of these roofless holding pens—used to confine stray animals in the eighteenth and nineteenth centuries—often display the same thick, blocky dimensions as a foundation, complete with vertical interior walls and a rugged, battered exterior. In most cases, however, town pounds are fully exposed rather than interred in the ground, giving us a chance to study the building method that continues even today to support so many of the fine old houses and barns all across the New England countryside.

WELLS

IN THE AGE of rotary and hammer drilling, the trick of stoning up a water well isn't in much demand anymore. But its technique is still useful in at least one important way. At many construction sites, the addition of fill to the landscape surrounding buildings often threatens nearby trees with suffocation by burying their roots too deeply. Shallow wells are frequently stoned up around these trees, so that the original grade level in the immediate vicinity of the trunk can remain intact.

These structures are built exactly the same way as the old stone wells. They are circular retaining walls, continuous inside curves whose member stones show their narrow ends in the face while their wider ends are anchored in the mass. Properly built wells are among the longest lasting of all dry stone structures, because their stones are locked in a 360-degree arc from which no escape is possible. Pressure from all sides merely squeezes the stones more tightly against each other over time, and the fat-end-in, narrow-end-out design keeps individuals from popping loose.

The principle of well stoning applies to any inside (concave) curve, whether it is continuous or not. Because the length of its face is less than the length of its corresponding backside, many, even all, of its face stones can show their narrower ends, just as in a well. Finally, although wells are retaining walls, you don't need to build them with the same amount of backing mass as in a foundation or a noncircular retainer. The initial excavation, if its radius is half again the length of your longest stone plus the width of the finished opening, should give you enough room to back up the well's structural members with enough mass to hold them in place.

SINGLE-STACK WALLS

THE SINGLE-STACK, or *farmer wall*, is a ubiquitous icon of the old New England landscape, yet it is only occasionally constructed today. As its name implies, this type of wall is for the most part only one stone wide (see the opening illustration in chapter one)—although builders would not hesitate to lay widths of two or three stones in occasional spots where such doubling up created more stability for the next course. Single-stack walls were almost always built to fence in livestock, usually sheep, at heights of 4½ feet or so. Some were topped off with wooden poles or other brush to present a more intimidating barrier. This was also the type of wall most favored for the delineation of boundary lines.

Because of their narrow configuration, single-stack walls function poorly as storage structures for stone, but they offer at least one advantage wider walls cannot match: speed in construction. Skilled builders with ready access to stone could erect many feet of these walls in a day's work, which is one reason why New England acquired so many miles of stone wall in such a relatively short time. No other method of enclosure can quite equal the single-stack's combination of economy, efficiency, and endurance.

The waning of the single-stack's popularity among contemporary builders and their clients is regrettable but not mysterious. Single-stack walls are a practical architectural response to a set of circumstances that has passed, and their aesthetic qualities, though valued by those who cherish the New England countryside, don't particularly appeal to contemporary taste, which favors a wider, more formalized style of stonework. Single-stack walls, after all, have no faces to speak of. You can see daylight in the joints between their stones, which makes them appear somewhat less substantial than thicker, double-faced walls. Moreover, they require fairly regular maintenance, a concept that flies in the face of modern assumptions about New England stone walls and tends to relegate them even further to second-class citizenship.

Nevertheless, the single-stack wall has not yet entirely vanished, if only because so many homeowners find themselves moved to repair or reconstitute existing examples on their properties. Builders who undertake this style should be aware that its technique, while comparatively primitive, calls for some special considerations both in design and execution. Unlike double-faced or retaining walls, for instance, which assign stones of certain shapes to certain segments of the structure—the face, the cap, a corner, the interior—single-stack walls are much less discriminating. In a way they are nothing *but* structure, merely a balanced stack that succeeds aesthetically more by virtue of function than artifice.

To begin with, single-stack walls have no binding interior mass within which stones of various sizes and shapes can be laid and clutched on all sides. Because of this, their composition is more strictly graduated than in other types, from the very large stones of the base to the smallest on the cap. Whether any of a single-stack's members present faces or particular alignments to the eye is of no account: All that matters in a single-stack wall is that each succeeding course of stones presents nooks or surfaces where the next can firmly perch. Since a large stone will generally support a slightly smaller one more readily than one of equal or greater girth, the consistent segregation of stones by size in single-stack walls gives many of them the appearance of battering, but this is an outcome of structural practicality, not artistic intent.

The one-over-two/two-over-one rule applies to the single-stack wall just as to other styles, but with a difference, for the absence of an interior mass or a defined face means each stone must be independently balanced when it is laid. Particularly in the lower courses, stones in a single-stack should rest on at least three points, as widely separated as possible, and not all on the same supporting stone. The weight of each stone should be centered over the middle of the wall, so that shifting and settling will not encourage it to slide or drop to one side or another too readily. Side-to-side pressure does help to bind the stones of a single-stack together in a finished piece, but this should not be counted on in construction. Builders who try to stabilize dubious placements by counterbalancing them with other stones or propping them up with chinkers only guarantee that inevitable future problems will metastasize to perfectly sound sections above and beside the original error. When single-stacks deteriorate, they do so in chunks, developing gaps like the missing teeth in an old hockey player's grin. Notwithstanding their reputation for longevity, they are actually the most delicate of traditional dry stone structures, a fact that was borne home to Derek one summer day when a couple of his visiting grandsons spent the afternoon amusing themselves by pushing stones off long sections of the old single-stacks on his Hopkinton farm.

RETURNS

RETURNS ARE THE short lengths of wall leading away from certain corners, usually on retaining walls, that finish off an otherwise exposed end by "returning" into the ground of the higher grade. They also form the containing sides of stairways built into larger walls. What distinguishes them is the way their bases appear to rise while their caps remain level, an illusion created by the rising grades in which they are embedded or the steps they seem to climb.

As with stairways, it is not necessary to excavate the entire footprint of a return to the depth of its lowest point, but because the pressure of its settling will make it want to slide downhill, you should make sure that the first three or so feet are dug in to grade. This will provide an anchor that helps keep too much pressure from accumulating against the corner itself. Past three feet, the base of the return can begin to rise, in steps, along with the grade of the bank, just as shown in the cutaway drawing of our set of *exposed* (meaning without containment by returns) stairs on page 91. Cutting the bank itself into steps as you excavate upward rather than laying the return's base on sloping ground will also help to reduce its tendency to slide.

There is a temptation to regard returns as decorative afterthoughts and thus to build them less heavily, and with less care, than more prominent sections of the wall. This is a mistake, for the wages of carelessness are no different here than elsewhere, and deftly built returns (particularly those enclosing steps) add visual pleasure to stonework that is disproportionately greater than the amount of space, or labor, they require.

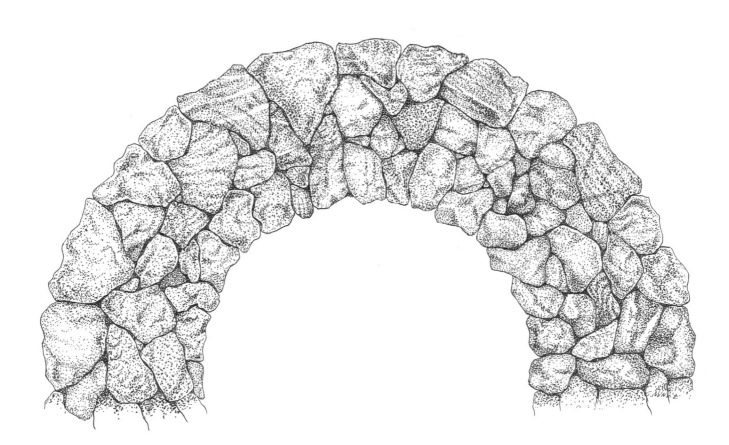

Curves

Traditional New England wall design tends to favor the straight line, but contemporary practice has expanded its repertoire to include arcs, curves, and even fully circular constructions. These are not only useful as elements of a design, but also enormously pleasing to contemplate all by themselves. The arrangement of unyielding stones in a flowing, curving line creates a visual marriage of stability and relaxation that makes all kinds of aesthetic statements possible, from practical response to surface variations in the land, to fanciful forms that express a delightful idiosyncrasy. Perhaps no contemporary builder has exploited the potential of the curve more thoroughly than artist Andy Goldsworthy, whose designs for dry stone constructions, like the Storm King Arts Center wall, in Mountainville, New York, feature an astonishing series of loops, switchbacks, and sweeping curves more characteristic of a river than a stone wall. Goldsworthy's deliberately exaggerated stream of stone slaloms its way through trees, runs freely up and down slopes, and even plunges into a lake at one point, emerging on the opposite bank as though uninterrupted. The Storm King wall's triumphant playfulness makes it simultaneously an embodiment of traditional craftsmanship and a penetrating comment on the power of stone walls to define or transform our view of a landscape.

For designers like Andy Goldsworthy, the poetic use of the curve is circumscribed by little more than the limits of imagination, but builders with more modest (and more practical) aims must also take one important structural consideration into account: the great difference, from a construction standpoint, between an "inside" (concave) and an "outside" (convex) curve. To understand how this distinction affects builders, consider the humble donut, the shape of which is essentially defined by two concentric circles.

Imagine for a moment that your task is to build a donut shape out of solid, freestanding wall; a continuous circle with faces showing both on the outside circumference and around the inside of the central "hole." Of these two concentric faces, which will be easier to build? If you answered, "The inside one," you're correct. Why? Concentric circles (or any portion of them) grow ever wider as they radiate outward from the center, so their lines of circumference grow longer and longer, and require more and more stone to fill them up. This means that the face of any convex curve, whether or not it constitutes a complete circle, must be composed, *on average*, of stones that present their fatter, broader ends in that face, and their narrower ends to the inside, where the available lateral space shrinks steadily the farther in you go. Outside curves are thus prone to structural instability, because their individual face stones are less likely to be locked securely in the mass of wall—too many of them are positioned with their wide ends exposed. Over time, settling will tend to squeeze these stones out of place, but a builder's opportunity to compensate for this fundamental weakness—by mixing in face stones of even or increasing thickness from front to back—is severely restricted by geometry. Outside curves must therefore be assembled with extra care in both picking and placement, for they will respond to compromise or carelessness with swift deterioration.

On an inside curve, however, the situation is reversed. Here, most of the face stones must present their narrower ends to the air, and the chances that settling will expel them are significantly reduced. This is why inside curves are so much more stable than convex ones. (See the section on wells in this chapter.)

Of course, any freestanding wall that forsakes straightness will present you with back-to-back inside *and* outside curves, just like our theoretical donut. The principal trick for building such a wall is to design it with enough width to allow the use of the deepest, most stable stones available in its convex faces. Remember, too, that the more acute the curves you design, the more pronounced this phenomenon becomes. Therefore, the most successful outside curves, in terms of longevity if not of drama, are those that arc as gently as your design will permit. The sharper they turn, the more difficult they will be to build and to maintain. Retaining walls, with their single faces, are much less complex. In these cases, if you have a choice of inside or outside curves, choose an insider. They're easier to build and much less likely to develop trouble later on. It's worth noting that Andy Goldsworthy, enthusiastic proponent of radical curves, considers the eventual deterioration of his constructions to be a part of their life as works of art. Given the structural vulnerability of the outside curve, that's a healthy attitude to take.

STEPS

THERE ARE NUMEROUS ways to construct stone steps. They can be overlapping or offset. They can be configured within retaining walls or exposed on one or both sides. Steps can climb evenly from bottom to top or rise in stages to wider landings, as they often do in houses. They

CUTAWAY OF EXPOSED STEPS
A cutaway drawing of simple overlapping steps, showing an excavation filled with small stones, tightly packed. The steps are "exposed" (without containment by returns), and the excavation itself is roughly stepped upward into the bank.

can run straight into a wall, rise parallel to its outside face, curve as they go, or feature angled changes of direction on the way.

From the standpoint of the builder, the first significant decision about steps is whether they will be overlapping or offset; in other words, whether the leading edges of the stone or stones of any given step will rest on the back ends of the stones in the step below. This choice has considerable effect on the shapes you'll be able to employ: Overlapping steps require component stones of relatively equal thickness, whereas offset steps offer much more flexibility in terms of selection, because they do not rest on one another and can therefore be set into the underlying material at any depth that allows the bearing surfaces of their member stones to meet one another at the same level. Offset steps, then, are a bit less fussy to build, but overlapping steps have their own advantage: They tend to lock together and stabilize themselves more readily than do offset steps, in which each level is structurally separate.

Second, builders should have at least a rough idea of their proposed stairway's width and height, in order to calculate the number of *step-stones* they'll need. Steps that are three feet wide, for example, will generally use up at least two stones per tread and often three. If the stairway must rise 45 inches, it will take five 9-inch steps, or nine 5-inch ones, to get to the top.

Whatever their configuration, stone steps should be built heavily. As a general rule (there are always exceptions), individual step-stones should have an average weight of one hundred or more pounds to help ensure stability under traffic. Step-stones that are securely trapped, either by succeeding levels or by the sidewalls of the stairway, can run a bit lighter. Still, a primary concern must be the absolute immobility of each stone where feet will land. Rocking, shifting, unstable steps are dangerous, and few things are as unforgiving as a fall onto their implacable hardness.

If people watched where they were going more diligently than they do, step building would be easier, and the irregularities that make New England fieldstone a pleasure to contemplate might be as freely displayed in steps as in other constructions. But people cannot be counted on to pay attention to topographical eccentricity, particularly when it comes to steps and stairs. Their feet tend to make certain assumptions, a fact that step builders should take to heart. One of those assumptions is that the *rise* (a step's height, the distance from one level to the next) will be consistent from step to step on any given stairway. This does not mean builders in stone must follow the 6½- to 8-inch standard rises that carpenters use for wooden stair construction, only that whatever rise is used remains pretty much the same for the entire stairway, say within an inch or so. Fieldstone steps can accommodate some imprecision but not too much—a 6-inch step followed by a 10-inch cliff will cause half the stairway's users to trip or to lurch abruptly downhill.

People's feet also assume that a step's *leading edge*—where the rise meets the *tread*, the step's bearing surface—will be essentially continuous. This means that builders must be careful to match the leading-edge corners of stones in the same step against one another as tightly and carefully as possible, leaving no gaps large enough to swallow an unwitting toe or heel. Of course, stones that match nicely side to side all the way to the back of the tread are preferable, but gaps away from the edge can be filled with smaller material that cannot be easily dislodged. Out at the edge, where most people put their weight, the stones must meet.

This requirement alone reduces the number of viable steps you can expect to find in a given run of random fieldstone, and when you consider that step-stones must also have the right weight and thickness as well as (relatively) flat surfaces, the difficulty of locating enough of them for a substantial stairway becomes apparent. Depending on the extent and variety of your source, this is a case when a pallet or two of preselected stones from a commercial supplier may prove more cost effective than an open-ended search for these special shapes. Examine any stone you may be thinking of purchasing this way very carefully, however, not only for proper size and shape, but for color and texture, which may be quite different from the supply you already have on hand. In terms of design, steps can succeed even with some deviation in patina or stone type from the wall of which they are a part, because the form of their construction already departs from that of the main mass, but you should be certain before you build that the difference is one you can live with.

Stone steps are not just a series of graduated, traffic-bearing levels presenting flat, tightly fitted surfaces for climbing. They are also retaining walls, built to hold back the hidden mass of material behind and above each of their component steps. This is a helpful idea to keep in mind during construction, because with each new set of treads you are actually laying the base for what amounts to a new retaining wall— a base that is also a cap! All the rules for effective layout of retaining walls therefore apply to the building of steps, from the determination whether or not you will need to create a stone-filled trench underneath the bottom step (or first several steps) to the necessity of backing up each new course of step-stones with carefully fitted and leveled interior packing to prepare a stable new base for the next set of treads. Individual step-stones, in addition to the pounding they must absorb from foot traffic, are also more vulnerable to frost and water because they are not nearly as well clamped in place as are ordinary wall stones. Therefore, most stone stairways need to rest on reasonably substantial beds of fitted rubble, not only for stability, but also for drainage. This means the excavations for steps can be extensive, particularly when they are designed into high retaining walls where they must occupy much more depth than does the wall itself in order to have room for enough treads to reach the higher grade. These excavations, however, need not be dug to the level of the bottom step underneath the entire run of stairway— they, too, can be graduated upward as the stairs rise, as long as each succeeding step is supported by perhaps ten or twelve (or more) inches of

WIDE SET OF STEPS SHOWING INTERWOVEN CORNERS AND RETURNS

A wide set of overlapping steps built into a retaining wall. Note the way the outside step-stones of the bottom set of treads extend underneath the corners of the returns and the breaking of joints between step-stones from one tread to another, as though they were laid in the face of a wall. Both the wall and the returns carry a hard cap of heavy, flat stones.

underlying stone. In occasional cases, the substrate may be so dense and the step-stones massive enough that this much excavation is unnecessary or impossible.

When steps are to be built into and contained by a wall, both wall and stairway should be constructed at the same time, with the base, steps, corners, and sidewalls (or returns) rising simultaneously. This allows the builder to weave together components as he or she goes, using one end of a bottom step-stone to support a corner of the opening in the wall, for instance, or allowing a step with a ragged, unfittable side to hide itself partly in the return, leaving its more cooperative side exposed. Each new layer of work should begin with the placement of a set of steps, after which the backing, corners, and returns may be built up to match.

There are two simple tricks that seem to make the composition of steps a little easier. First, select one outstanding step-stone that will serve as a kind of anchor for the entire tread. If the tread is only one stone wide, you're on to trick number two, but stairways wider than sixteen or so inches will usually need multiple side-by-side step-stones in each tread. Step-stones do not have to be square, though of course they're easier to fit together when they are. In preparing to build, you'll find it helpful to note potential step-mates, stones that will sit well side to side, even as early as the hauling process. The anchor stone should be placed somewhere near the middle of your proposed step, and set to the height and level you want—with adjustments, if need be, to the supporting base material underneath. (A supply of flat shards comes in very handy for this operation.) When the steps are to be overlapping, make sure that your anchor stone rests solidly on the tail end of a stone or stones in the previous step, even if it must be shimmed up to reach the desired rise. This is the second trick: When laying these large, heavy stones into the stairway, do not try to anticipate the underlying adjustments you may have to make by guessing. Instead, just place the step in the spot you like and then, using your bar or simply by lifting, hold the stone in place while you adjust, add, or remove supporting material. If the stone is very heavy, you can do this one side or end at a time. When the stone is settled in position, pack any remaining spaces as tightly as you possibly can to give the step uninterrupted support. (If you can't see underneath it, reach in from behind with your hand to make sure you're not leaving little caves.) Now, with the anchor firmly ensconced, you are ready to place the other step-stones on either side, the anchor serving as a kind of mark for the height and level of the step as a whole.

Random New England fieldstone will offer many potential step-stones that appear *almost* ideal for your purposes but not quite. They may be too thick, too thin, or too oddly shaped to lay tightly against others. They may be flat on one side and impossibly rounded on the other. In many instances, you'll be able to devise strategies to cope with these difficulties, particularly after a little practice. Even more than with other kinds of dry stonework, steps demand patience, and the will-

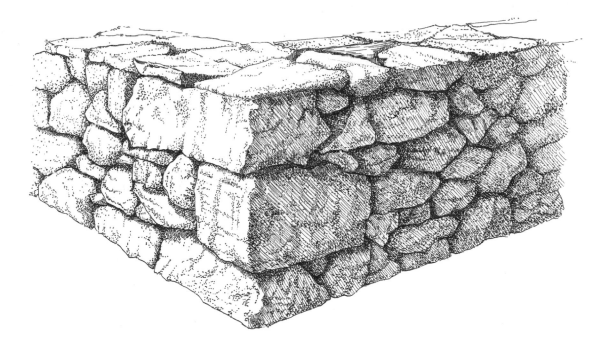

ingness to try again and again until you achieve the functional and aesthetic results you're after.

CORNERS

NEATLY LAID CORNERS are among the most satisfying and beautiful forms dry stonework can take because, like other special structures, they are focal points that invite more scrutiny than do uninterrupted runs of face. When they are successful, corners have a way of imposing

CORNER WITH CROSS-HATCHED PLACEMENT
The stones of this heavily built corner show, in somewhat exaggerated fashion, the staggered, cross-hatched placement that knits together the two converging faces where they meet and end.

order on the motley randomness of New England fieldstone that graces the entire structure. On the other hand, a sloppy or unstable corner can degrade the whole wall's visual impact with equal effect. Since corners of one kind or another are required in a great many types of walls, and as components of numerous other specialized forms (such as butt ends, foundations, and returns), familiarity with their construction is particularly useful for any wall builder.

The principle of a well-built corner is that its exposed stones are alternately gripped primarily in one, then the other, of the corner's converging faces, so that if you were to examine only one of those faces, you would see what appeared to be a (relatively) long stone over a (relatively) short one over a (relatively) long one, from bottom to top. This kind of dovetailing appears in fine furniture, of course, and in the corners of brick or quarried stone buildings—although with considerably more precision than one can expect from unshaped fieldstone. Nevertheless, the principle, as in the interwoven fingers of clasped hands, is the same.

Careful selection and scrupulous placement are the keys to a good corner. As you might imagine, a typical supply of New England's glacial detritus offers relatively few stones in which parallel flat surfaces are combined with convenient right angles. Builders must therefore teach themselves to see corners in stones where they may not be immediately apparent and to imagine combinations of un-square stones that will produce a corner when they are laid alongside one another.

Potential corner stones should be identified and reserved throughout the process of hauling and initial layout, not just because of their rarity, but also because good corner stones are always excellent builders, or even thrufters, and the temptation to use them up in other sections of the wall will be strong.

The anticipation of placements at least one step ahead is also critical: Each layer of a corner construction should be arranged so that it offers a level, stable surface for the next stone or stones, never a sloped or acutely uneven bed that requires shimming or other improvisational compensation. Corners are particularly unforgiving of chinking and trapping, practices that should be confined, when they are used at all, to the uninterrupted stretches of the wall proper.

Of course, corners do not necessarily have to be built at ninety-degree angles: The same care in selection and placement can produce clean, well-balanced corners at more obtuse or more acute dimensions. Remember, though, that anything less than sixty degrees or so will require you to construct what amounts to a sharp vertical edge, a form considerably more difficult to build in terms of both selection and placement.

BUTT ENDS

BUTT ENDS ARE the exposed conclusions to freestanding double-faced walls, which end (or begin) at full height, and they are among the trick-

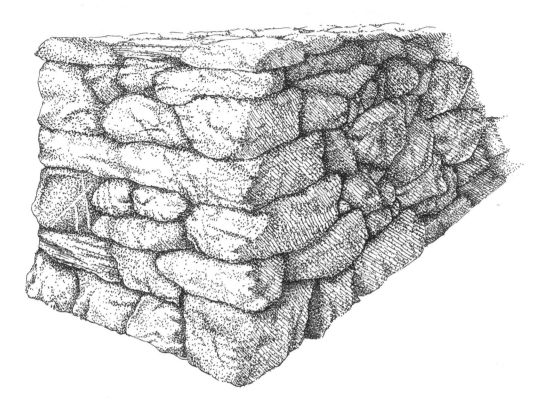

This well-built butt end features a binding through-stone about two-thirds of the way up. In the wall's face, to the right of the near corner, you can see the character-istic "stepped" pattern of heavy stones that helps to contain side-to-side pressure exerted by the body of the wall.

iest configurations most wall builders must contend with. For one thing, they require a pair of corners—a difficult proposition under any circumstances. But they present another structural challenge, too, for a butt end is more than simply a tidy termination point. It is also a retain-ing structure—a bookend, in a way—for whatever lateral pressure may be exerted by the wall of which it is a part. The usual stresses on double-faced walls—uneven settling, face stones dislodged by internal collapse, and the like—are compounded at a butt end by the potential of the whole structure to relieve itself of tension by pushing the end away and eventually toppling it. Therefore, butt ends must be built more carefully and a bit more heavily than other sections of the wall.

One way to conceive the structure of a butt end is to imagine it as a set of overlapping steps, incorporated within the wall and visible (to a practiced eye) as the graduated backside of a retainer. None of the stones in this arrangement should be dependent for stability on its neighbors to the right or left—they should all be laid with absolute solidity on the stones below, so that the pressure of their settling will be directed primarily straight down. This requires the careful selection and use of stones with largely parallel top and bottom surfaces, both in the face and internally: Butt ends are not good places for experiments with eccentric fitting or odd, irregular shapes. Particularly in the spaces between opposite corner stones that do not meet, be careful to fill the gaps with stones that are deep enough to be well gripped inside the mass. Butt ends will spit out shallow chinkers faster than almost any other kind of structure.

The cross-hatched, offset laying of corner stones in a butt end is particularly critical, and particularly fussy, because the amount of leeway in the face of the butt itself is restricted by the width of the wall. This means that some stones with perfectly good corners or nicely matched parallel surfaces will be useless because they are too long, or too short, to fit the available spaces constructively. In spite of this difficulty, builders must still seek to lay the largest, most stable corner stones they can locate in butt ends, and if opposite corner stones meet one another in the face of the butt, or even (halleluiah!) run all the way across and show *both* corners, so much the better: Through-stones in a butt end are exceptionally stabilizing. If you are fortunate enough to have a few such paragons on hand, spot them into the butt every two or three courses, so their binding influence will help secure other courses made up of two or more stones.

PILLARS

THE ARISTOCRATIC FORMALITY of a pillar lends a certain elegance to the entrances to driveways or private access roads, recalling among other things the age of the great nineteenth-century summer estates in New Hampshire towns like Dublin, Wolfeboro, and Tamworth. Although pillars can be constructed to stand freely, they are more often used as termination structures for the stone walls that flank vehicular portals. Smaller versions can be incorporated in garden walls or as components of formal landscape designs. Dry-laid pillars are usually square (round ones are possible but exceedingly difficult to build without mortar, unless they are very large) and almost always somewhat wider than the walls to which they are attached, a detail that helps to give them a more finished look and also provides the additional bulk necessary to sustain the structure's height. Pillars look well when they are about half again as tall as their attached walls, but more modest dimensions can succeed, too, just as long as they are neither too squat and stubby nor too skinny and elongated.

Pillars comprise four corners, or four butt ends, with all the attendant care in picking and placement those constructions require, and with extra attention to the inclusion of thrufters in the faces of each side, as well as the interweaving of corner stones. Their interior packing should be exceptionally fastidious, relying as little as possible on stones smaller than a fist. When incorporated into a wall, the transition joint between wall and pillar should be crossed by long stones as many times as possible, both internally and in the face. Finally, because they exert more pressure on a smaller footprint than most dry stone structures, pillars are more likely to topple to one side or another as they settle. Because of this, they often demand a solid base of crushed stone even if the underlying material is stable enough to bear ordinary wall work.

STILES

FOR SHEER INVENTIVENESS, few of the specialized forms dry stonework takes can equal the stile, a construction whose sole purpose is to allow human beings easy passage through or over a wall while simultaneously confounding livestock. Stiles were often built of wood, sometimes as roughly framed steps hurdling a wall and sometimes as elaborately gated interruptions of its line. But they were made of stone, too, in a number of different forms.

The simplest stiles are what Eric Sloane calls *grikes*, merely a narrow slit between stones in a single-stack wall, through which people can squeeze without climbing. Creating a grike is a little more involved than using one, however, since it obligates a builder to fashion butt ends on either side of the opening. Sloane's drawing (in his *Diary of an Early American Boy*) shows these ends built heavily, of fairly squarish stones solid enough to resist the pressure of the wall at their backs without toppling into the gap.

In very thick double-faced walls, stiles can be installed as built-in steps, running straight in, up, and over. Sometimes stone or wooden posts were anchored right in the top of the wall, on either side of the steps, and a bar or gate set between them. Step-stiles can also be built as cantilevered arrangements, using long, flat stones set well into the wall's mass and protruding to form a primitive stairway parallel to the wall's face. Curtis Fields built such a set of steps, not as a stile but in a large retaining wall at his home in Vermont, where the characteristic fieldstone of his neighborhood—broken, relatively flat slabs of ledge— offered plenty of long, narrow step-stones. Cantilevered steps are wonderfully simple and quite striking visually, but they require a considerable mass of stone to anchor them properly. At least two-thirds to three-quarters of each step-stone's length should be buried in the wall, and the steps nearest the top, where there is less bulk to counterweigh them, should be massive enough to bear traffic on their own without tipping. Ideally, when cantilevered step-stiles are built into double-faced walls, they should be composed of stones long enough to protrude on both sides, so that each stone provides two steps, matched and balanced. If the wall is too thick or such through-stones are unavailable, you may find it necessary to offset them within the wall to give each step-stone enough anchorage. In these cases, the inside ends of the steps can be built to pass one another, over and under, the way thrufters do, or the stile itself can simply change direction, running down the opposite way.

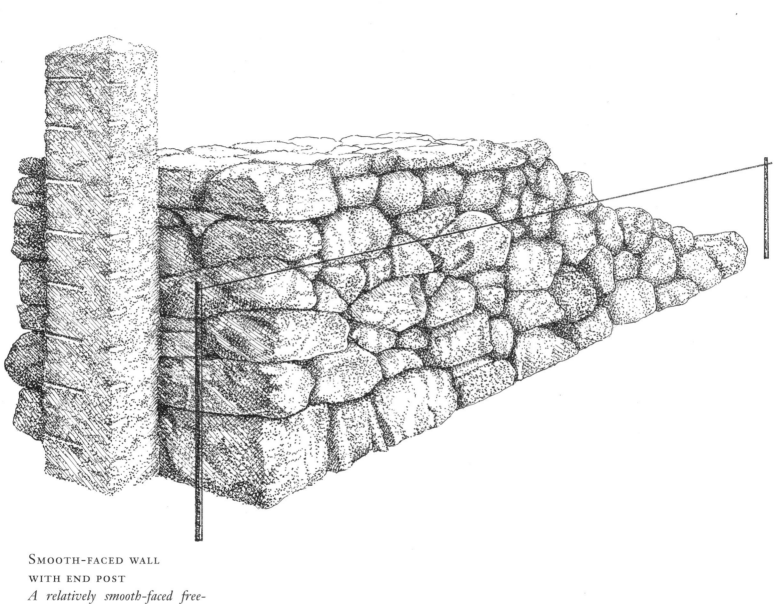

SMOOTH-FACED WALL
WITH END POST
A relatively smooth-faced free-standing wall is terminated with the formal look of a granite post.

RHYTHM *and* TEMPERAMENT

6

WAYS OF MANAGING THE WORK

Some may know what they seek in school and church,
And why they seek it there; for what I search
I must go measuring stone walls, perch on perch;
> —ROBERT FROST, *"A Star in a Stone-Boat"*

STONE WORK IS slow and contemplative, as much about looking as lifting. In the early stages of practice, however, it is likely to be supremely frustrating. What does it feel like to learn to read? Most of us long ago forgot the mystery of indecipherable letters on a page or our struggle for the trick of balance that first allowed us to ride a bicycle. There is a similar epiphany in wall building—after a while, a long time or a short time, depending on your willingness to persist, you'll get it. Here are some things to keep in mind during that initial period of self-instruction.

It has been our experience that people who focus on process rather than results learn to build more effectively. Impatient enthusiasm for visible progress is a fine approach to woodcutting or raking the lawn, but in stone work it leads only to error and frustration. That is why it is helpful, when starting out, to worry very little about what you actually accomplish. Instead, concentrate on doing properly what you are trying to do even if it takes numerous false starts and experimental placements before you succeed. Remember, too, that mastery of the craft involves more than merely technical understanding. Part of what you are teaching yourself is a way of working, of parceling out your energy and managing the physical activity itself, almost the way a runner does.

Stone wall building has a kind of rhythm to it, a thoughtful, measured ritual of looking, moving, looking; stooping, lifting, moving; placing; and looking again. This sequence of actions, repeated over and over, induces stupefying ennui in some people, and purposeful satisfaction in others. Still, you can improve your chances of developing a taste for the work by approaching it as a methodical sequence of tasks rather than a formless exercise in spinning gold from straw that begs for the intervention of Rumpelstiltzkin. Because every run of New England fieldstone is a little different from the last one, and every builder's perception of shape slightly different from the next one's, dogmatic prescriptions for an orderly working rhythm are all but useless. The important thing is to find your own and to practice it at a pace you can sustain. Here are five techniques that will help:

- *Pick the stone for the spot, not the spot for the stone.* In other words, work from the wall to the pile, making selections from your supply to match available spaces in the project as they appear rather than seeking places for individual stones that attract your attention. Beginning builders develop an appreciation for well-shaped stones almost immediately, and while this is a good thing, it also beckons you toward inefficiency, in two ways. First, you'll inevitably wear yourself out with unnecessary lugging. Even experienced builders have been known to waste their effort in futile searches for spots that don't yet exist, just to find a home for a particularly enticing stone. Second, working backward (from the pile to the wall) almost guarantees that you will dispose of the best material you have too quickly, making the less compliant bulk of your supply much more difficult to use.

Efficient use of your effort makes an enormous difference. The old-timers expressed this principle by saying, "Don't pick up any stone that you don't lay in the wall," or "Handle each stone but once." "A hole for every stone, and a stone for every hole," snaps the redoubtable Ian Cramb; "What you lift, you build." (Note that he says "a hole" first.) You may not be right every time you think you've matched a space with its ideal stone, but in the long run you'll build much more efficiently if you start each sequence of looking, moving, lifting, with the immediate needs of the wall in mind rather than an impulse to use a particular stone.

- *Try to train yourself to remember more than one available space.* The hardest stone to find is the *one* you want. By memorizing three or four of the gaps you have to fill, you multiply the chances of seeing what you need when you turn from the wall to the pile. Don't rush. Stand and study the wall until you have several possibilities in mind. Then look for any of the stones that match. This is a skill that improves dramatically the longer you practice.

- *Move on if your work area temporarily defeats you.* From time to time, vision and imagination fail so utterly that no amount of study can unlock the secrets or supply the needs of the particular stretch of wall you're facing. In that case, abdicate. Walk down the line ten or so feet and start over in a new spot. Resume the excavating you didn't finish or go haul in some additional stone. Change the focus entirely, until another day freshens your eyes, or inspiration returns. If you're working with others, exchange areas and look at someone else's problems for a while. My main partner for the last fifteen or so years has been my sister-in-law Stephanie, and we have developed a nearly unconscious habit of relieving one another, section by section, when things bog down. (We also maintain a standing mutual permission to remove and replace each other's most awkward or unsound placements.) Even so, there are days when nothing works, and the best thing to do is simply stop.

- *Aim for steadiness rather than speed.* Productivity in stone wall building is a function of efficiency and stamina, not aggressive exertion. That is why so many of the greatest builders are able to continue in the trade well beyond the age of peak physical vigor. Their experience has taught them how to avoid wasted motion, so that everything they do results in actual progress. Perhaps even more important, their practiced ability to anticipate placements several moves ahead of the one they're making at any given moment means much less time spent studying the wall or their supply of stones. In time, you will see how it is possible to continue to move and to study wall and pile simultaneously, establishing an uninterrupted mental and physical rhythm that will surprise you with its effectiveness, and allow you to keep working for longer and longer periods without exhaustion. Much of the fatigue brought on by stone work is indeed mental, a result of too much time spent poring over difficult spots, trying to fit a stone that won't willingly go anywhere, or working in brisk bursts separated by uneven spells of distracted inaction. A slow and steady rhythm avoids all this and builds the wall much faster, too.

- *Avoid needless force.* Perhaps the most peculiar notion beginning builders occasionally develop is the idea that sound placement can be achieved by slamming or pounding stones into spaces where they do not fit. Particularly common in men (surprise!), this habit is as futile as it is unnecessary. It's an exercise in cognitive dissonance to think that material that has endured the unimaginable pressure exerted by a mile-high glacier will meekly yield to the puny violence offered by human hands. More to the point, slamming is an enormous waste of energy, a sure way to shorten your patience and your day. In addition to their other qualities, stones possess non-negotiable willpower: Either they *will* go into a given space or they *will not.* Gentle, careful placement will produce precisely the same result, and in the long run will do it faster and more frequently than any amount of grunting ferocity.

"A man learns something about himself when building a wall," amateur builder Roger Griffith declared in John Vivian's *Building Stone Walls*. One of the things men, or women, may learn about themselves while building a wall is the depth of their aversion to the whole business. My brother Tim, for instance, was a clever woodworker, of admirable patience. He could sand a small object for hours to achieve a particular softness in its finish or carve tiny pieces of doll furniture inlaid with fragments of mirror. But he could not build a stone wall. The process struck him as impossibly unmethodical, and he succumbed to frustrated paralysis whenever he tried it. Dan Neville, the meticulous builder who runs our barn restoration service, reacts the same way. He can elevate an enormous timber-frame structure inch by inch until it resumes its original shape and configuration, and painstakingly rebrace and rejuvenate it over many weeks, yet the confrontation with a pile of random stones horrifies and depresses him. There's no obvious reason why Tim or Dan could not have been skilled wall builders. They simply lacked the temperament or the inclination to soldier on until the process began to make sense. It's tempting, in a book that seeks to convince people that stone work is something they can do for themselves, to argue its universal appeal. But our experience tells us something else; that for some, wall building is a suffocating, unendurable bore. Nevertheless, beginning builders should not be dissuaded by the results of their first efforts: With stone work, you even have to practice in order to know that you hate it!

> When you look at the first few square feet of completed wall, it almost never looks right. But do not let this put you off. I get this same feeling. It will look better as you progress.
> —Ian Cramb, *The Art of the Stonemason*

Here is an astute piece of advice from a man who spent much of his career restoring fourteenth-century Scottish castles. For some reason, partially completed stonework is profoundly unsatisfying to contemplate and can lead you to believe during a project's early stages that you are doing something wrong, that your design is flawed, or even that, after all, you didn't really want a stone wall in the first place. But there is always a moment, sooner or later, when the immature jumble coalesces, and your wall achieves form and presence. Some walls take longer than others to reach this point—occasionally, full development isn't visible until the piece is capped and finished. On our own projects, we have noticed many times that just the removal of the final guide strings improves a wall's appearance, as though the simple act of declaring the work complete produced completion all by itself. Part of this phenomenon, of course, is that the absence of strict visual reference lines allows the wall to emerge on its own and assume full responsibility for its relationship to the surrounding landscape. But while the project is still under construction, its own raggedness, and the abstractions imposed by profiles, stakes, and strings, will distract you from seeing it fully. In this respect the act of building is an act of faith, all the more reason to pay attention to process before progress. The beauty of a good wall is an accumulation of small excellences, a deft, pleasing, personal pattern that can only be achieved one stone at a time. Development of a working rhythm based on this fact will not only improve your capabilities much more quickly, but will also put you in the best possible position to enjoy the work for its own sake. This, in fact, is an important (and perhaps historically unique) aspect of contemporary approaches to the craft.

There is no disguising the redundancy and rigor of wall building's activity, yet many people find it strangely soothing. There are even "stress-reduction" stone work weekends being offered in some places, opportunities for interested amateurs to pay for the privilege of skinning their knuckles on someone else's wall. Those who take to stone work find in it at least two redeeming qualities, aside from the well-advertised satisfaction of seeing the finished product.

The first is a fascination with shape and the relationships among shapes. New England fieldstones are often described as "round," "rounded," or "glacially worn," terms that imply an obstinate uniformity, as though they were hardly more useful for wall building than marbles or soccer balls. This allegation seems to have arisen only by comparison with more accommodating types of stone, in other parts of the world where wall building is traditional. But even though New England's stones cannot offer the obvious constructive advantages of Kentucky's quarried limestone or the shattered shales and schists of the British Isles, they are very far from being invariably spherical. Instead, they are characterized by a profuse diversity of forms, textures, colors, and sizes, hardly describable in any simple, all-inclusive way. Assembling coherent and stable structures with such stone draws builders into minutely detailed considerations of the proper places for every kind of shape, from a loaf of bread to a manhole cover, a process that people with certain organizational or artistic temperaments find enthralling. It is not uncommon for New England wall builders to become nearly obsessed with shapes, able to recall for months or even years a particular favorite they once encountered, or one they needed but could not find. My aunt, Ruth Owen, once returned from a hiking trip laden with stones she had lugged down from the top of a mountain, just because their shapes appealed to her so irresistibly. Her only regret, she said, was that she had not been able to carry more.

The second attraction is the pleasure of the activity itself, particularly for those who do not make a habit or a profession of manual labor. This is not to claim that a few hours spent hoisting stone offers an instant, soul-restoring balm of sweat and accomplishment to the weary office worker. Wall building's existential satisfaction, if it can be called that, takes time to discover and to refine, just like the skills of observation and construction all beginning builders must learn. "Comfort is the opposite of pleasure!" a Hasidic religious philosopher once said. Stone walls are hardly comfortable to build, but the pleasure they afford is visceral and addictive, the physical equivalent of gazing into a fire or producing a perfect sentence.

"Stone work does not demand a lot of thought," concludes writer John Jerome. Yet his book *Stone Work* argues a more complex view, by example if not by intention, for it is a book full of thoughts, enclosed, like an overgrown, flower-strewn hayfield, by the stone wall its author builds, contemplates, and returns to throughout the book's casual, observant ramble. Perhaps it is true that a right-brain activity like wall building makes relatively few demands on the thought processes we regard as industriously productive, yet it is also true that the repetitive simplicity of fitting stones leaves acres of one's mental field clear for other activity. This can take the form of nonlinear meditation capable of producing surprising insight about all sorts of things or simply a state of alert restfulness free from the fidgeting and inattention that afflict our overstimulated modern minds. Stone work does not *demand* a lot of thought, no. But it *allows* a lot of thought—enough, in John Jerome's case, anyway, to write a book about. A good day of wall building can leave you in a most agreeable condition—physically exhausted yet mentally refreshed—and this condition, so different from the state most of us find ourselves in at the end of a day, is part of the reason builders love the walls they make.

The reverence for stone walls is also a residual longing for the genius loci, the spirit of place that we have systematically banished from our thoughts and plans but which our hearts still recognize and crave. Many of the people now crowding into the old places left by New England's generations of farmers can sense the echoes of animation still inherent in the way those farmers shaped the landscape and the built environment, yet they are in no position to experience their predecessors' intimate daily relationship with that landscape. The ability of latter-day New Englanders to achieve a true connection to place is therefore handicapped, no matter how much we may long for such connection. "Past and place are inextricable," writes architect and teacher Norman Crowe; "A place that is important to our past must rise above nostalgia in our consciousness lest it become merely quaint." Because the building of stone walls simultaneously evokes both the imagery and the engagement of the past yet also produces useful structures for the present, its practice is deeply satisfying to those who wish, as Crowe puts it, to "sense a resonance between the new and the old, between what came before and what has been added or has evolved."

The temperament that loves wall building is one that seeks order and balance, that loves symmetry and interdependence, that does not mind doing things slowly. It is a temperament that appreciates the small variations among many apparently similar objects, and finds interest in arranging them as tightly as possible within a prescribed area. If you know what Hamlet meant when he said, "I could be bounded in a nutshell, and count myself a king of infinite space," you may well be suited for the rhythmic, accumulative repetition that is wall building.

7

NOTES *on* DESIGN

THINKING ABOUT WALLS IN THE LANDSCAPE

The difference between our age and the past is in our way of seeing.
—JONATHAN HALE, *The Old Way of Seeing*

WHEN WE VISIT a client to discuss a new wall project, the first questions we hear are often about design. How tall should it be? How wide? Should it run straight or curve? What about some steps? Should it be battered? How will it end? Where?

These questions sometimes make us a little uncomfortable. We are not designers in any formal or commercial sense, and the adaptability of dry stonework to so many kinds of spaces and intentions offers considerable leeway for personal expression. Our own preferences, after all, may not come close to pleasing others, who in the end must live with whatever we build. One thing we do know, however, is that the best answers to these questions rarely appear as a result of abstracted approaches to "style" or "design." Stone walls are more likely to succeed as design when their *function* is clearly visible. Therefore, the

SHAKER VILLAGE
CARRIAGE HOUSE WITH WALL
IN FOREGROUND
This view of the Canterbury Shaker Village carriage house demonstrates one way in which stone walls can balance, contain, and extend a composition of land and buildings. (After a photograph by Scott Swank.)

question we ask our customers is this: What do you want your wall to do?

Sometimes this question seems vaguely impertinent. Many people in New England want a stone wall just to have it, to occupy the empty space between a house and a road or to tag along beside the driveway like a good dog, legitimizing ownership of the territory with its presence. The iconography of stone walls is so powerful that it is sometimes assumed they are self-justifying as elements of a landscape, and even capable of authorizing entire schemes of layout and composition. Many designers in the landscaping business now center their plans around stone constructions of one kind or another, a tradition that threatens to become a cliché. (Their enthusiasm, however, has been a boon to wall builders everywhere.)

Yet the overwhelming preponderance of landscape design today is sterile, gratuitous, and generic, endlessly redundant with its tidy islands of bark mulch, its clusters of obedient shrubs, and its stranded accent stones, beached and defeated like small, unfortunate whales. Lifelessness is its principal characteristic, not because landscapers are incapable of creating functional or inviting places, but because the marketplace for their profession has taught them that contemporary landscaping's primary purpose is to express propriety and inoffensiveness rather than pleasure, curiosity, playfulness, mystery, or any other individuating quality. In this respect, landscaping has followed the dominant trends of home design and home siting, which are now ruled almost entirely by real estate markets and the automobile. Social and economic developments that have transformed houses into commodities and work into a quest for assets have profoundly altered our relationships to place, and the loss of former certainties about where we "belong" expresses itself in everything from the self-help industry to the historic preservation movement. Even so, the marketplace doesn't know, or care, where we are, so it eventually makes all places look the same.

The many people who treasure their surroundings and have worked hard to preserve the traditional integrity of the New England countryside might find such a complaint disheartening or even offensive. Nevertheless, they should not be surprised. Unlike previous tenants of New England's rural landscape, most of us live on the *surface* of our environment, as though it were a stage set, rather than *in* it, as the wall-building farmers did. Even those who make their living out of direct contact with the land—loggers, certain contractors, the few who still farm—do so at some remove; "sustained," as architect Paul Shepheard puts it, "by our machines." The character of our relationship to the landscape, whether around our homes or elsewhere, is thus fundamentally altered, seduced into carelessness and arrogance by the chain saw, the backhoe, and the bulldozer. As our ability to sweep away and refashion the form and content of the natural world grows more casually comprehensive, we are more and more alienated from its growth, its rhythms, its life. They go on anyway, of course, but we cannot see. Instead, we mistake our dominance for understanding, and allow it to trivialize and diminish things we might otherwise consider precious: a hillside, a field, a tree. Because we can do anything we want, we do, and the restrictions and necessities that forced older shapers of New England's landscape to respond to the land itself no longer apply.

None of this, by the way, is to claim environmental superiority on behalf of our dead ancestors. In many ways, we are much more fastidious than they. We would not allow a tanner to set up his smelly operation in the middle of pretty Hopkinton village, for instance, or a sawmill to choke the Blackwater River with tons of sawdust. Every family no longer has its little bottle dump out in back of the house somewhere. Older attitudes toward the development and disposition of land included an almost infantile faith in the earth's capacity to cleanse itself. "Where does the smoke go?" I asked my mother once, when I was small. "Away," she said. I suspect she would give a different answer to that question today, when even pollution has become a tradable commodity.

But what does all this have to do with stone walls? It's passing strange, and more than a little ironic, that our heightened sensitivity to the effects of environmental contamination, whether by exotic chemical compounds or the ordinary ugliness of urban sprawl, should be accompanied by such apparent indifference to the uses, and the very aspect, of the land around the places where we live. But because we no longer derive our substance from that land on anything like a direct or daily basis, we have lost a crucial link that connects the things people build to the places where those things sit. This is the loss that makes it possible for stone walls to fail, as "design," in a way they never could before, and it is the reason we must be careful to avoid placing new stone walls in the landscape with no other intention than to provide adornment.

In New England, where dry stonework is a cultural identifier as well as a landscaping option, walls *can* be a visual antidote to the placelessness that afflicts so much contemporary design, and a great many avocational wall builders have found that it is possible to recapture some sense of real engagement with landscape by designing and building their own. The inherently personal expressions that find their way into the forms and patterns of dry stone walls also help to banish the generic and make a place one's own. But stonework's power to invoke specificity in the sense most valued by those who admire the region's antique walls is dependent on something designers and homeowners sometimes neglect. In order to succeed as landscaping, stone walls need a job. With an obvious function, they more often than not perform nicely as visual and symbolic connectives to the older landscape features around them or, in the immediate absence of those features, as references to more historical landscapes not far away. (This, of course, applies only to structures built of weathered native fieldstone—imported or freshly quarried stone is by its nature a stranger to New England's visual tradition.)

The power of New England stone walls to define or enhance a

landscape design is inherent in their function, for without something to do, stone walls are hardly more effective or evocative than the next Weeping Cherry or Victorian gazing ball. This is one of the reasons antique stonework seems to integrate itself so well with intelligent contemporary landscaping. The exposed foundation of a long-gone barn, for instance, transformed into a partially enclosed space of grass and flower beds, or a restored dooryard animal pen whose great jagged blocks of granite guard roses and daylilies instead of livestock, preserves essential reminders of former use that enliven a landscape with meaning. Even if the original function of such old stonework is mysterious, its very idiosyncrasy resists generic categorization and stimulates curiosity that invites a closer look.

The list of jobs that stonework can do is long. Stone constructions can determine not only the way one looks at a space, but also the way one moves around in it. They can enforce a sense of privacy or invite people to enter. They can protect flower beds, provide places to walk or to sit, hold off the wind, and keep the deer from the garden or the baby from the road. Stone walls can be trellises, benches, tables, paths, or portals. In addition to these and other concrete tasks, stone walls can also work to organize and unify the abstract aspects of a composition, a function particularly suited to the needs of contemporary designers. Keeping these capacities in mind will make the answers to questions about form, style, and location much easier to discover.

Where should a new wall stand? In many cases, the best way to place a wall where it will look "right" is to follow patterns of use; in other words, to distinguish separate areas from one another according to *their* functions. This is why walls around gardens, between field and forest, or street and lawn, most often work. The traditional placement of stone walls in the New England landscape is an expression of intent for the spaces they enclose or separate, and this principle is as relevant to contemporary landscaping as it was to the farmers of generations past.

Another way to find the right place for a new wall is to imagine it in concert with the lines and flow of existing landscape features or of nearby structures. Stone walls do more than simply organize a landscape by enclosure and division: They also unify compositions of land and buildings by serving as visual intermediaries between the two. This is a job for which they are uniquely qualified, because they are structures made out of the land itself. Their dual nature, as both natural forms and artificial arrangements, initiates what theorists might call a "dialogue" between the found and the built environments, and this dialogue is a major reason why people find New England's old walls so attractive, and why stonework remains so desirable among homeowners and landscape designers.

Stone walls can unify developed landscapes in several ways: by rootedness, by extension, by repetition, and by linkage. Good designs frequently combine two, three, or even all of these elements in a single wall, a principle that is repeatedly demonstrated in the antique constructions around New England's villages and farms. The quality of rootedness is perhaps most evident in foundation work, never more dramatically than under the downhill sides of certain old barns, where great freestanding walls emerge from the higher grade to complete a level surface for sills. Any building on a visible foundation of laid stone seems more securely rooted to the spot, as though the land approved the building's presence by lending its support. Foundations are not the only sources of rootedness, however. Almost any stone wall that is visually proximate to the lower extremities of a house or other building will create this impression, from a retainer that binds the raised grade on which the building sits to a simple planter that conceals a section of exposed concrete. Even a low, decorative freestanding wall, following a brick walk from the front door to the driveway of a modern home, can convey a sense of solidity and connection that architecture alone cannot always achieve.

Impressions of rootedness are particularly strong when they are augmented by extension, that is, when the lines of a building are picked up and lengthened by a wall. If our old barn foundation, for instance, does not end where the building stops but continues in the form of a retaining wall or becomes a ramp that drops gently from the barn door to a pasture below, the roots of the barn appear to reach farther than the building itself, and its integration in the landscape is even more intimately established. Similar effects occur when smaller garden walls run parallel to a home and then beyond or when retaining walls (often with a set of steps) are used to create a level apron of grass or garden in front of or around a building that sits on uneven terrain.

By repeating lines already present in a building, stone walls ratify its geometry in powerful but subtle ways. That is why we will often set the level of a wall's cap to match the clapboard line of a house, for instance, even if the ground beneath the wall rises or falls away. Walls that maintain a uniform height relative to the grade on which they sit have their own kind of power, but when they adjust themselves up or down under a level cap to mimic the lines of a building, they are much more likely to help unify compositions of land and structure. Repetition can also be very effective in another way, as a reflection of a building's outside dimensions. Stone walls that parallel one side, then turn and follow another, spread the visual impact of a structure's shape across a wider area and help settle it in the landscape. This kind of repetition need not be exact to be effective: The sharp corner of a building can become a gentle curve on its echoing wall; separate sections of the wall do not have to be equidistant from the building; and the lengths of given sections may only approximate or hint at the lengths of the facing structure. Poets call this principle *assonance*; an imprecise rhyme that carries an echo nonetheless.

Linkage occurs when stone walls are used to connect different areas of a landscape (or its various buildings) to one another or to frame them as a group in some way. This principle is familiar to anyone who has driven by old farmsteads on New England's country roads, admiring the classic proportions of house, barn, and outbuildings across the top of a continuous roadside wall. Walls that run between or behind buildings, that provide access from one place to another, or that combine different forms in one structure (such as a retaining wall that rises above its bank to become a freestanding bench on the upper side) all act to link together separate areas.

Any of these considerations can be useful in deciding where to locate a stone wall most artfully, but as a practical matter, location is frequently influenced by topography. Particularly around new homes, where excavation and final grading have left awkwardly steep banks vulnerable to erosion; on excessively wet or uneven terrain; or on sites where outcroppings of ledge, trees, or other natural features are already present, choices for the placement of a wall may be predetermined or significantly restricted. The topographical peculiarities of a site may also suggest locations or encourage conceptions uniquely suited to themselves. Some of the most arresting designs for new stonework come about as a result of imaginative interaction with a landscape's natural elements, as Andy Goldsworthy and others have made startlingly clear.

Once you know where you want your wall to be (and why you want it to be there), a host of new decisions clamors to be made, all having to do with the style and dimensions of the wall itself. While these decisions are in many ways personal ones, they also carry consequences in terms of both design and construction. I'll start, quite arbitrarily, with the question of height.

One of the pleasures of writing this book has been the liberation it has provided from the political protocols of the contracting business. It's always enjoyable to talk to people who love stone walls, whether or not they're prepared to pay the substantial costs of having them built, but every now and then the design recommendations our customers request create conflicts between our true opinions and our wish to avoid the appearance of enlarging a project for the sake of commerce. This sometimes leads us to a certain amiable evasiveness in conversations with clients who need a little assistance deciding exactly what they want in a wall. So the opportunity to temporarily discard unhelpful diplomacy in favor of frank (if equally unhelpful) preference should not be allowed to slip away.

The truth is, taller walls are better. Most dry stone walls don't become genuinely interesting until they reach heights of thirty-six to forty inches or so, when their forms, configurations, and patterns start to have real impact on the landscape from multiple perspectives. The genteel, twenty-four-inch garden wall has its place, to be sure, but taller walls appeal to us more directly, for a number of reasons. First, you can see them at a distance, and therefore whatever part they play in the larger scheme of a landscape is more active and more profound. Second, they create both backdrop and mystery; the first for the elements or areas in front of them, and the second for the hidden things behind. Taller walls also correspond more closely to the dimensions of the older stone structures that are their inspiration, and so participate more immediately in the development and extension of New England's established visual tradition. Beyond all that (and entirely aside from anything to do with design), they're much more fun, and more satisfying, to build.

Three- and four-foot walls, of course, are not appropriate for all circumstances, sad as it is to say. They may be out of scale with other elements of a design or too dominant to perform the kinds of integrative functions noted above. Tall walls can be awkward, too, if they aren't long enough. Forty inches of freestanding wall needs at least thirty or forty feet of run, or it tends to look like an afterthought or something unfinished. (Exceptions to this caveat include places where the wall is intended to close a gap between other large elements or structures, such as buildings, trees, or sharply inclined banks of earth.)

When the project is a retaining wall, decisions about height are at least partly dependent on the size of the bank to be contained. Most retaining walls should rise to within a foot or less of the spot where their caps meet the higher grade, but beyond that designers have some discretion. Retaining walls look fine when the bank is graded down slightly to meet them, but they can also run even with it, or slightly above, in order to show a bit of facing on the inside of the upper level. If the area above the wall is an active one—a patio, say, or an elevated stretch of lawn beside a house—the retainer can also continue upward as a freestanding sitting wall or something even more substantial, as long as the structure is built heavily enough at its base to support the extra weight.

In dry stone wall work, width and height are a little more codependent than in other kinds of masonry, because dry walls need proportional amounts of mass to hold themselves together. The higher you build them, the thicker they must be. Taking into account the site conditions, and the type and quality of stone to be used, we will typically lay out the width of a freestanding wall at two-thirds to three-quarters of its height. A four-foot-high, double-faced wall, then, will need at least thirty to thirty-six inches of width and will usually build (and stand) more comfortably at the higher figure. A New England fieldstone wall is notoriously ill-tempered if it senses inadequate bulk relative to its height and will sooner or later collapse as peevishly as a toddler in a supermarket.

This means that designers must be willing to accept a certain amount of width for every foot of height they intend to build, a fact that holds just as true for retaining walls as for freestanding ones, since the base of a retainer, though largely hidden, still must occupy a footprint wide enough to bear its load. There is one exception, however: the old-fashioned single-stack wall. This type, because of its larger stones and quite different method of construction, can run somewhat higher than fitted double-faced walls without requiring as much overall width. For those whose taste runs to the rustic, the single-stack is a design option that should not be overlooked.

Should your wall run straight or curve? This choice is nearly always aesthetic rather than practical: Well-planned walls will fulfill their functions whether they run from one end to the other as the crow flies, arc gracefully in a half circle, or meander back and forth a few times along the way. Straight lines tend to recall the familiar layout of the old New England landscape a little more directly, and they are perhaps more powerful in evoking a sense of orderliness. Curving walls, on the other hand, soften and vary a composition too regularized by gridlike patterns, and they can be enormously useful on sites where the natural landscape is too flat and characterless to offer much interest on its own. In terms of their surroundings, straight walls are more likely to create impressions of determination, expediency, and decisiveness, whereas curving walls are frequently better suited to response, to acknowledgment, and to suggestiveness. Straight walls give instructions; curving walls, persuasion.

What about some steps? There are two reasons to consider adding sets of steps to the design of a wall project. First is the obvious one: the need to create openings and access from one place to another where everyday traffic must be accommodated. But steps serve a larger purpose, too, by creating relationships between separate places even when actual passage between them is seldom required. The formal entrances to many old (and new) houses show how this principle works, expressing symbolic invitation and welcome to the world at large while the family comes and goes almost entirely through the kitchen entrance off to the side. Steps (and other openings) between areas divided by stone walls function in a similar way, helping to unify a design and give it a focal point that draws the viewer in.

Should a wall be battered, its face (or faces) tapering in as they rise?

The argument is made by some builders that this method produces a much more stable structure and is therefore preferable or even required. Much of the old and new writing on stone walls also prescribes battering as a basic element of correct technique, particularly for freestanding types. But Colonel Frederick Rainsford-Hannay's description of the ancient brochs of the Shetland Islands, which featured immense dry walls almost forty feet high, indicates that the builders who laid up these circular fortresses as long as 1,800 years ago (to defend themselves from Swedish and Danish pirates) had no trouble with vertical building. "The first 25 feet," writes the colonel, "would be built on a 'batter,' [and] the next 13 feet of height would be vertical." From an engineering standpoint, a 13-foot vertical dry stone wall capable of enduring from the second century to the twenty-first is probably not significantly flawed.

Our view, then, is that battering is a design choice only, and that correct construction makes a lasting wall whether it is battered or vertical. If battering were a necessity in dry stonework, we would see a great deal more of it than we do in antique New England walls. Whatever structural stability may be gained by the technique is too negligible to matter in most cases, and those who prefer their stonework straight up, as we do, shouldn't hesitate to build it that way. There is one aspect of battering, however, that isn't much remarked on—it uses less stone. Perhaps that is one reason why the method was never exclusively embraced in New England, where the ancillary objectives of wall makers often included using as much stone as possible to get it out of the way.

The question how best to end a wall is often among the thorniest of design decisions, perhaps because there are so many ways to do it. Walls can square themselves off into butts, gradually taper or shrink away to nothing, or maintain their height as they disappear into a rising grade, the way a return does. They can terminate against granite posts, large single boulders, or great, square pillars of laid stone, taller and thicker than the wall itself. These choices are all structurally workable, so the decision comes down to preference and to coordination with the wall's prevailing style, whether rough and rustic (boulders), refined and estatelike (pillars, posts), or something in between.

The larger, murkier question of "style" extends well beyond the ways walls can be terminated, of course, and often requires considerable thought. Quite apart from matters of placement, dimension, and function, there is a vast number of variations in the ways stonework can be made to look, and different writers have defined these building styles in different ways. Eric Sloane arranges them in terms of construction, drawing distinctions (quite literally) among thrown walls, laid walls, and chinked walls. Susan Allport separates older traditional styles from what she calls "walls of affluence," which feature the tighter, flatter, formalized appearance produced by contemporary professional masons. Others define style as little more than an operative function of the type of stone being used. Most of these definitions essentially break down to a distinction between "agricultural" and "estate" attitudes toward design, the first characterized by utilitarian roughness and the second by self-conscious craftsmanship. In practice, however, there are so many variant combinations of these two qualities that common definitions of style in New England dry stonework must remain either unworkably broad or, like descriptions of certain colors, maddeningly elusive. The solution is to find a model of the style you like, whether you discover it in photographs and illustrations or in exploratory travels around the countryside. Once achieved, awareness of the stylistic variations that are possible will never leave you and will inform your own building as you develop a personal style inspired, but not imprisoned, by the model you admire. Just as in the act of building itself, your selection of a design scheme should ultimately reflect an instinctual preference. If it does, your stonework is far more likely to enrich the landscape rather than merely decorate it.

The utility of a design, or its inspiration, is not always immediately apparent. There is a man who lives some distance to the east of us, in a nice old house very close to a busy road. For quite a few years now he has been plugging away at a massive wall along what appears to be the entire roadside frontage of his property, a distance of several hundred feet. Driving back and forth to our own jobs, Stephanie and I have watched his progress with more than a little skepticism. His idea of scale can only be described as gigantic, for though his wall is four or five feet high, it is made of stones so large that only two or three courses of them are needed to reach the top. We have seen him from time to time, wrestling these monsters onto the wall from the bucket of a front-end loader. The stones are madly misshapen, arranged in a kind of double-stack, with no attempt to create a face. Furthermore, the stones are "new"—unweathered, freshly dug out of the ground at some nearby pit or construction site. The wall's hulking design, its bizarre proportions, and the buff plainness of its color are all anathema to antique stonework snobs like Stephanie and me.

Yet the longer this wall has stood, and the more of it there is, the better it seems to look. For one thing, it has absolute integrity. It is the realization of one individual's vision, uncorrupted by imitation or by enslavement to "traditional" design notions. This much was visible from the start, but mere defiance of convention is not enough: It can make a thing absurd, or triumphant, with equal ease. Now, however, that the builder has brought his creation past the house and started along the remaining section of his frontage, this unique wall's function is finally clear, and in that clarity its form makes perfect sense. That is why, before much longer, this wall will be a kind of triumph.

The wall is there to defy the road. Not to politely suggest the difference between a private space and a public thoroughfare, as a more delicate wall might do, but to defy the road on the *road's* terms, as massively and constantly as the twenty-four-hour frenzy of tires and engines that passes not fifty feet from where this wall builder and his family live and sleep. If looked at in the context of its builder's house, the wall is thuggish, swollen, and relentlessly out of proportion. If looked at in the context of the road, it is just about right—maybe even a little on the small side. It is a psychological barrier and as such, a brilliant design. I've noticed, too, that its stones are already beginning to weather. In a few more years someone will come along and think, "They don't build 'em like that anymore." But they do.

REPAIR *and* RESTORATION

8

TECHNIQUES OF IMITATION AND THE
IDEA OF RENEWAL

Restoration is renewal—an effort to mend the world—or else it is not worth doing. — HOWARD MANSFIELD, *The Same Ax, Twice*

Knock down the old gray walls. — BADFINGER

WHAT IS THE difference between repair and restoration? Put a little too simply, it is the difference between patching today's hole and delaying the appearance of tomorrow's. In a broader sense, repair is mere upkeep, the maintenance of a certain degree of physical wholeness, the piecemeal reconstitution of an aging wall's most distressed sections. Restoration, as Howard Mansfield has eloquently established, involves something rather more complex: a renewal of purpose, of spirit as well as substance, that restores not just the object in need of mending, but the mender as well. In technical terms, many of the methods of repair and restoration are similar, but it's helpful for builders to know before-

ENTRANCE TO THE
LONDONDERRY POUND
The entrance to the Londonderry (New Hampshire) town pound, an early nineteenth-century stone structure that replaced the original 1730 wooden enclosure. The stone lintel was carved during an early restoration effort, in 1933; more extensive rebuilding took place during the mid-1990s. The pound is approximately thirty feet square, with walls that average around six feet in height. The opening is placed at the structure's right-hand corner, and the end wall to the right of the gate shows the foundation-like construction typical of many stone pounds.

hand which task they are setting out to accomplish, because the distinctions between the two can have considerable effect on the ways a project is planned and executed. Since basic repairing is, on balance, a more straightforward process than restoration, we'll start there.

Stone walls can fail for a number of reasons, including poor building, changes in site conditions, ice and water damage, or the accumulation of shiftings and settlings that accompanies advanced age. Perfectly sound dry stonework can endure only so many of New England's relatively minor (but regular) earthquakes before its weak spots begin to crumble. Open winters (those with little snowfall) aggravate the potential for frost heaves that can throw a wall's base courses out of alignment. Trees fall across them, children climb on them, and scrambling animals topple their capstones. Accumulations of leaves and other debris can collect water inside a wall, destroying its capacity to drain properly, then prying stones apart when the water freezes. When the failure is at or near the top of a wall, repairs are relatively simple regardless of the specific culprit—just replace what has fallen, making sure to stabilize the stones underneath if they too are partially dislodged. But when problems occur at or near the wall's base, and larger sections begin to bulge, lean, or spill out, a little detective work can help ensure that the repairs you make are lasting ones. This detective work should take place while you are dismantling the section you're going to rebuild, which is one reason, but not the only one, why the dismantling should be done with care.

The structural interdependence of a dry wall's component stones is much more pronounced with New England's glacial rubble than with other, more cooperative types of material, so to remove a stone from a New England wall is, as often as not, to remove the security of a second stone, or a third, or a whole group. Furthermore, even fallen sections of wall will often continue to support those still standing, so that neatly surgical excisions of bulges and blowouts are rarely possible without additional dismantling. This is why you should remove the offending section stone by stone, from the top down, rather than haphazardly digging your way into the mess from the middle or the bottom, where your enthusiasm is likely to trigger unnecessary collateral destruction. Your goal is to clean the wound completely, leaving sound sides and a solid base from which to begin again. Repairs nearly always involve the removal and replacement of more stone than the troubled section itself contains, particularly in double-faced walls, where the dismantling of one bad side will frequently cause the opposite face to cave in as its supporting internal mass is pulled away. The first rule of repairing, then, is to anticipate more work than the problem may seem to require but to do your best to minimize the inevitable.

As you remove the stone, take a good look at each new layer you reveal. In the face and at the sides of the gap you're creating, note the number of decent thrufters the wall contains. If there are very few or none, you may already have discovered the reason for the failure. Look, too, at the wall's interior packing, particularly to the sides of the excavation where you've cleared away enough of the loose stone to be confident that the remainder will stay in place. Is the interior tightly packed, or are there gaps and large crevices between or among the backers and the face stones? If there are, two possibilities exist: that the face is peeling away from the core, usually because it is not sufficiently anchored by thrufters or through-stones; or that the interior itself was carelessly built, allowing it to collapse over time and to build up pressure on some sections of face while falling away from others. Make sure that you remove enough of the interior mass directly behind the face to be rebuilt, so that the deep tail ends of your new thrufters will have enough space.

When you near the bottom of the dismantled area, examine the last few face stones very carefully. Often, the instigator of a blowout will be a single stone, dislodged by uneven settling, bad placement, and/or pressure from behind. You may find that this stone has not even entirely left the wall, but has only slid slightly out and down, becoming trapped in the avalanche caused by its expulsion, like the petrified victims of Mount Vesuvius. When blowouts occur in a rough V-shape or a kind of conelike scoop, there is almost always one unlucky stone at the bottom of the disaster, waiting to be discovered.

A potentially more troublesome cause of wall failure is damage or misalignment at or underneath its base. Uneven settling on a footprint that is too wet or too soft, dubious selection or placement of outside base stones, water action that undermines the material below, or the expanding roots of trees growing too close can tilt entire sections out of line and even topple them. The base stones under older work or single-stack walls are often very large and partially interred, but unless they still offer a reasonably level surface for your repair work, they too will have to be removed and reset, a process that can obligate you to dismantle substantial sections on either side of the offender. When you have excavated such a stone, refill the hole with crushed granite or small stones tightly fitted, not with soil. This will help prevent the same sort of problem from recurring, particularly where traveling water is the cause. Don't hesitate to replace soil with stone over as wide or deep an area as you think necessary or are willing to expose, and if a base stone turns out to be a cheap seducer, banish it and find a replacement. Someone else's laziness does not have to become your headache.

Repairs invariably require extra stone, in fact, and not just because some of the material already on hand may be unusable. Since it is virtually impossible to build the same wall twice, even casual repair work calls for additional supplies of stone to ensure an adequate variety of sizes and shapes. Furthermore, you'll often find that given repairs consume a volume of stone that is noticeably greater than the amount originally in (or out of) place. Most New England walls spread out and loosen up as the years pass, and though that gradual relaxation may be dramatic in some cases, or nearly imperceptible in others, it always adds a certain amount of empty space to a wall's interior. The much tighter fitting of a fresh repair occupies that space with stone once more, a circumstance that calls for extra bulk even if the shapes and types of the original supply are plentiful and of high quality.

The issue of matching comes up in one way or another on almost every repair or restoration project. If you're interested in duplicating the texture and disposition of standing sections adjacent to a repair, so that new work blends harmoniously with old, you must consider not just the stone itself, its shapes and types and patina, but also the characteristic building style of the older work, and even the degree to which its original condition has deteriorated. Such thoroughness isn't necessary in all repair work, of course, but when it is, there are some tricks and short cuts that may help.

The Laurentide Ice Sheet and its predecessors in glaciation were not equal-opportunity stone distributors. For one thing, the underlying bedrock they encountered during successive periods of advance and retreat varies significantly from place to place across New England, the result in part of tectonic collisions that, among other things, created the Green and White Mountain ranges. Geologist Robert Thorson has temptingly described that bedrock as "broken shards stirred into a magma pudding" (and when Thorson talks about "shards," he means chunks of the earth's crust the size of whole states). Alternate eras of melting and sedimentary layering associated with New England's geological and volcanic formation further blended the types of stone already present, or introduced, in local areas. After that, the glaciers clawed and ground their irresistible way across it all, humbling the mountains and transporting vast quantities of stone to new locations. But not usually very far from their sources, surprisingly enough—Thorson points out that most stony material trapped in the ice only moved a mile or so from the place where it was picked up.

As a result of all this, our renowned landscape seems to have experienced an extraordinarily chaotic brand of discrimination in terms of the varieties and conditions of stone strewn across any given part of it, and the legacy of this anarchic delivery system shows itself in the region's old walls. In some places, granite predominates, and in others, mica schist. Still others offer a scrambled succotash of these and a dozen more, including shales and sandstones, gneiss, slate, hunks of quartz and marble, bizarre conglomerates too strange to name, and even an occasional piece of volcanic tuff—the balsa wood of stone, brown and porous and light as a snowball. The composition of a stone supply may thus alter radically from one town, one farm, even one field to the next, a fact that can complicate the task of matching the specific variety of types in any given wall. Added to this challenge is the phenomenon of weathering, which occurs quite differently under varying conditions. The same chunk of granite, for instance, broken into five pieces and exposed for a hundred years in five different locations, will develop five distinct patinas. Stone that is mostly in sun or in shade, under trees or in open space, in wet or dry areas, even on the north or south side of a hill, will weather in accord with its particular environmental circumstances. Finally, stones of different types will react to identical circumstances in different ways, taking on stains or coloration, or supporting colonies of mosses or lichens, with greater or lesser enthusiasm.

Sometimes these interlocking variables conspire to produce hues and textures that are inimitable, especially when the stones in a given wall are largely or entirely of the same type and have developed a patina that extends uninterrupted across a wide stretch. Matching this sort of unified weathering with the new work of a repair can be difficult, but the task will be less daunting if you start with a definite idea of how much extra stone you really need. After you've dismantled the section to be rebuilt, make a rough estimate: If most of the original volume is still on site, you may be able to piece together the repair without too much trouble. In the context of matching, the only stone that matters is the stone that shows. Don't hesitate to substitute riprap or other unmatched junk stone for the weathered material of the fallen section's interior—you may be able to promote some of the old interior stones to duty in the face of the repair, particularly if the section has been fallen for a long time. When working on long runs of older wall, it is often possible to purloin single stones—the outstanding thrufters or builders you need—from other sections where they will not be missed or where they can be replaced with stones of less specific character. When these options are unavailable, the search should be extended to other sources where conditions (and the dominant type of stone) are similar. Take along a piece of the material you want to match, so you won't have to guess when you're examining the possibilities.

In many instances, mixtures of different kinds of stone give walls a more variegated, even mottled aspect. This circumstance can actually make matching a little easier, because a generalized appearance of variation will allow more leeway in individual selections than a uniform, explicit patina. If all else fails, remember that coming reasonably close is better than nothing—the conditions that produced the look you're trying to duplicate will eventually accomplish the same feat with your replacement stones, even if they aren't quite perfect at the start.

Color and texture are not the only considerations in blending new work with old, however. Most stone walls feature a particular pattern in their faces or configurations, the result of a collaboration between the preferred placement style of the original builder and the shapes of the stones themselves. Learning to see the lineaments of this pattern means, first of all, appraising the characteristic faces the builder chose to show. Are they relatively flat or roughly uneven? Is there a dominant theme in their shapes—mostly oval, for instance, squarish, or brokenly jagged—or does the wall contain a more random mix? Is there a pattern in the distribution of sizes, such as large stones at the bottom and smaller ones near the top? Is the wall capped in any distinctive way, with heavy, matched binding stones, for instance, or flat, thin plates? If this process is confusing, try thinking of the wall as a two-dimensional pattern made of nothing but elementary shapes. What are you seeing? Are they squares? Rectangles? Ovals, circles, trapezoids, cones? How many, proportionally, of each? Are some of the shapes indescribable composites? What is the range of their sizes? The more detailed your appreciation of the shapes and dimensions of stones in the face you are trying to mimic, the easier it will be to select appropriate extras for your repair work.

Not every repair job demands careful imitation of someone else's building style. The wall as a whole may be too distorted, or too carelessly built in the first place, for the effort to make any real difference. But when the original work has a recognizable pattern, and stylistic integration is your goal, the critical next step is to identify a few of the characteristic relationships among shapes favored by the previous builder. This can be done by examining undisturbed sections near your repair a little at a time and answering the following questions about the work:

- How fastidious was this builder about breaking the joints between stones of one course and the next? Are they regularly lined up right under the middle of the stone above, or sometimes, or often, to one side or another? Are running joints visible here and there, through two or three courses?

- Do the joints between stones fall consistently within a certain range of tolerances? Are there any oddly shaped cracks or gaps? Is the wall chinked?

- Are flat, rectangular, or oval faces always presented horizontally, or are they sometimes laid at angles or even on end? Are square, triangular, or other polygonal faces laid with one of their flat sides parallel to the baseline of the wall, or are they, too, placed at various angles?

- If the face is composed of stones with relatively flat faces, are those faces presented consistently straight up and down (or in conformity with the wall's angle of batter), or do they lean in or out now and then? How carefully did this builder align the planes of individual faces with the plane of the wall as a whole?

- Does the builder seem to have made an effort to create a series of level areas with each new *lift* of stone (or even just in certain spots), to carry the stones of subsequent courses, or does the work seem to be more improvisational, unplanned? Would its face look essentially the same if you turned the whole wall on end and observed it vertically, or are the stones laid in anything like recognizable layers?

In several important ways, builders must adapt their styles to the peculiarities of the stone they're working with. Wildly irregular shapes will not permit the arrangement of stones into neatly ranked courses, like brick- or blockwork, in which each joint is identically broken both above and below. Walls built with stones that are largely but not perfectly similar in shape and size foreclose many placement options because their lack of variety prevents certain kinds of improvisational compensation during construction. (This is the reason walls made of roughly dressed blocks and slabs frequently require shimming and chinking.) Anomalous individual stones or immovable boulders may force an interruption of established patterns in certain spots. Inexplicable changes in the quality or characteristics of a supply may instigate sudden stylistic shifts in the middle of a run. These and other variables can make it difficult to separate the preferences of a particular builder from the conditional influences of the stone itself, but certainty about the origins of a pattern is less important than a clear recognition of the elements that make it distinctive. In one way or another, every New England wall finds its form in a state of tension, between the organizational desires and the vision of its creator, and the restrictions imposed by the available material.

Finally, imitation of existing stonework occasionally demands that a builder attempt to integrate repairs with unfallen sections in various states of minor decay, a task that adds one more consideration to the list. This is the condition of the wall's overall path. Most older walls begin to wander a bit as time goes by, relaxing here to one side and there to another, easing away from the straight lines they originally described. (Some walls, of course, were never really straight in the first place, even though they were built from point to point without obvious curves or corners.) Repaired sections of such walls will often call attention to themselves by hewing too strictly to that long-ago layout—in other words, by being too straight! Therefore, in addition to matching stone and style, builders should take a good look at the wall from above while standing at one of its ends, to get a sense of the spreads, bulges, and leanings that have developed along its length. These, too, will often have a kind of pattern, and appreciation of its meandering will suggest slight curvatures or indentations you can build into a repaired section so that even the decaying idiosyncrasies of the older work will find an echo in your repair.

Except for this somewhat forensic form of imitation, the techniques of mimicry that match repair work to standing sections of original wall may also prove useful when your objective is the wall's full restoration. But restoration is a little more involved than the fixing of gaps and blowouts, not only because it is more extensive, but also because it calls for evaluations of purpose and impact simple repairs do not require. Real restoration nearly always begins with complete dismantling, partly to eliminate any possibility that structural weaknesses or distortions will be carried forward, but also, strange as it may seem, to clear the site of stylistic restrictions. Restoration of a stone wall may or may not seek to duplicate the specifics of a particular configuration or building style, but it should always aim at renewal of a wall's function and spirit, its relation to the landscape, and the strength of its presence. In the end, these are more important than the fussy replication of another builder's stylistic preferences, especially since restoration frequently replaces all or nearly all of the original work in a structure, thus removing any basis for comparison.

The first step in restoring old stone walls, then, is to find out as much as you can about how they worked when they were new and about the disposition of their original surroundings. This is sometimes impossible, particularly in cases of advanced deterioration, when extensive pilfering has taken place, or when the nearby landscape has been profoundly rearranged. Occasionally, an old photograph or other representation will turn up, and you'll have an indisputable reference. But there are several more direct ways to find useful evidence or, failing that, at least to educate your guess.

Always begin with a thorough examination of the site. Does the wall have sections that appear to be intact? In that case, you may have a model you can study and follow. Where sections are clearly not intact, is the missing stone right there on the ground? If not, the wall has almost certainly been robbed, and the stone will have to be replaced. But don't jump to conclusions based on a quick glance. With very old walls, particularly in the woods, fallen stones often disappear under leaf mold and forest trash and may not be immediately visible. One of the things walls do is collect windblown debris. That's one reason why the ground level so often appears slightly higher in the immediate area of an old wall. Excavation along its base will turn up the lost stones and usually expose an additional layer or two of base material that was plainly visible when the wall was new.

Next, do the wall and its surroundings have anything to say about original purposes? Are you looking at a rough-and-ready barrier between fields, a thickly mounded storage wall for the stones cast up by plowing, or more finely fitted work whose functions are decorative as well as practical? Sometimes, the landscape will answer these questions for you. In other cases, the stone itself can offer clues. Single-stack farmer walls, for instance, use less stone of larger average sizes than do double-faced walls, and their bases are often relatively narrow. These walls are most often found between pastures, on boundary lines, or along roads. Containment walls for waste fieldstone are much wider, sometimes with two or three lines of face on each side, successively hidden by expansion as continuous crops of rubble proved too abundant for the original dimensions. Walls like these were built next to cultivated acreage, often on the low side (it's easier to drag a full stone-boat downhill), and they seldom contain large supplies of very high quality building stone. The opposite is true of many walls laid up near dwellings or around consciously landscaped places like cemeteries, town greens, and public buildings. These walls were usually built of selected stones, so their proportional quantities of good builders, thrufters, corners, and stones bearing well-defined faces are often much greater.

When a wall has crumbled too much for its outline and dimensions to be clearly discerned, and even if the surrounding landscape is utterly altered, the stones themselves can thus act as guides for restoration. If you can be reasonably certain that most or all of the stone is still on the site, you can even approximate the wall's original size by calculating the total volume of stone per running foot and estimating various combinations of width and height that would require the same amount. (If the width of the wall's base is plainly visible when you expose it, one of those numbers won't be a guess.)

The clues in a disheveled run of broken wall aren't confined to matters of purpose and dimension, however. In broad terms, they may even offer information about building style. An unusual degree of uniformity in the sizes and shapes of face stones, for instance, can indicate that the builder aimed for a carefully regulated appearance, with courses ranked uninterrupted, in bricklike fashion. Undisturbed foundation courses canted slightly inward at the same angle all the way along the line suggest that the original wall was battered on one or both sides. The presence of a good supply of squared-off stones with parallel top and bottom surfaces near the end of a wall tells that its butt was once smartly tailored, with sharp corners and a solid, leveled appearance. A collection of thick (four to six inches), flattish stones scattered the length of the site and lying more or less atop the remains of the wall may be the remnants of a hard cap. By the same token, the *absence* of many outstanding builders and other specialized shapes often points to a more casual approach, to a wall more thrown than laid, or even to a "wall" simply allowed to accumulate over time, with little or no effort made at calculated arrangement. As your eye for stonework develops, the uses to which particular kinds of stone are put in particular kinds of walls will allow you to discover additional clues to the forms and functions of New England's ubiquitous, toppled masterpieces.

When the wall to be restored is partly or even substantially still standing, the number of suppositions you'll have to make about its original appearance and dimensions is of course reduced, and questions about building style are often answered before you begin. Nevertheless, a careful analysis of the structure is still in order, because stone walls, like old barns (or people, for that matter), can remain standing even though they're in terrible shape, and a true restoration aims to renew the wall entirely, not just visibly. Furthermore, nonfatal distortions in sections of standing wall frequently rearrange the relationships among stones thoroughly enough to obscure the intentions of the original builder, a situation that can complicate assessments of building style. In restoration work, the first decision to be made is whether any of the existing wall is worth preserving. That's why you should attempt to discover how truly intact those standing sections are. This can be done by examining the wall's line from one end (as noted above) and by evaluating the quality of the construction.

If the intended line of the wall is apparent, deviations due to heaves, bulges, or leaning should be easy to identify. (If the wall's line is confusing or obscure, try setting up a string just above one of its upper edges, or right down the middle, from end to end, to give yourself a reference point.) You can usually assume that sections that wander noticeably off the line are more or less structurally distressed and must be dismantled and rebuilt, not only to arrest the progress of their decay, but also to restore the wall's original form.

Was the wall well built? You may need to dismantle a bit to determine this, but there's nothing mysterious about what you're looking for. A well-built wall will have plenty of thrufters, a solidly packed interior, and some sort of consistency in its placements and in its appearance. The clear absence of any of these is grounds for rebuilding— fidelity to preservationist ideals need not extend its protection to mediocre or poor work.

In fact, relatively few restoration projects on old New England walls are materially enhanced by efforts to preserve original sections, unless they are in perfect condition, possess unique historical or artistic value, or carry personal significance of some kind. It is even possible to argue that the process of restoration is made more difficult when portions of the original work are allowed to remain. For one thing, its continued presence forces the same kinds of adaptations in stone selection and building style that well-integrated repairs require— except on a much larger scale. Perhaps more significantly, however, the positioning, configuration, and even the stones of preserved older work may restrict or eliminate certain procedures that result in a sounder, more consistent restoration. These procedures include shifting the wall's footprint, adding or subtracting width for reasons of structure or economy, expanding an inadequate excavation, and blending disparate types of stone. While they are not the only ways for builders to streamline the restoration process, they exemplify the kinds of imaginative adjustments you should be willing to consider as you contemplate your plan of attack.

The costly and time-consuming chore of disinterring enormous base stones is often a major part of restoration projects, made necessary because the stones have settled in ways that no longer allow stable placement at their outer ends, where the face or faces of the wall must rest. Sometimes there is no choice but to remove and reset them or to find more cooperative replacements, but in many cases, simply shifting the footprint of the entire wall to one side or another will allow you to restore the structure without disturbing its old base. One side of the restored wall will thus sit squarely in the middle of the line of half-buried stones, while the other will fall well beyond them on fresh ground, where you can create a trenched extension of the base filled with riprap, a far easier process than digging up rows of buried monsters.

The option to add or subtract a certain amount of width during a restoration project can solve problems of structure or of supply that may prove intractable for builders who insist on exact replication of the older work. If a wall has failed in part because it is too narrow properly to sustain its height, rebuilding it without additional width is quixotic stubbornness, not scrupulous restoration. And in cases where the old wall is clearly wider than it needs to be, a reduction of even six inches of width will effectively increase your supply of available material, sometimes by as much as several tons.

The restoration of retaining walls adds yet another consideration to the list, for in addition to evaluating quality and condition, builders must determine whether the wall's original excavation was sufficiently deep. Even well-built retaining walls are subject to untimely failure when their bases are too narrow to support the requisite amount of mass, a fact we saw demonstrated again and again at Maine's Acadia National Park during a training residency we conducted for the park's maintenance personnel a few years ago. Acadia's famed carriage roads are bounded by retaining walls in numerous places, built by crews working for John D. Rockefeller Jr. between 1915 and 1933. These are relatively young walls, but a number of them were in poor condition, not because they were badly fitted, but because they were built with inadequate bulk behind their lower courses. This condition is almost always the reason why old (and not so old) retaining walls begin to lean away from their banks and, eventually, to fall. Proper restoration of such walls should include the addition of enough new backing stone to create the kind of graduated damlike slope I described in chapter 2, a process that may require you to enlarge the original excavation in order to make room. If excavation is impossible, the restored wall should be laid out farther away from the bank on a new footprint that allows the necessary depth.

Finally, the difficulties of matching are also eased (somewhat) when restorers choose to dismantle completely before beginning to rebuild. The generally larger quantities of extra stone that restoration demands, as well as specifics of color, type, and texture, can bog down even the most conscientious efforts to duplicate the look of older work. By starting fresh, however, builders give themselves the opportunity to blend supplies of original stone with the new material they bring to the project, ensuring that the restoration's appearance will be consistent, whether or not it precisely replicates the older work.

These kinds of alterations and adjustments may seem oddly cavalier in the sacrosanct context of historic preservation, and perhaps in some cases they are. Certainly, there are plenty of instances in which the preservation of specific placement styles, design features, or even individual stones is integral to the identity of a piece of work. But the imprimatur of unmolested deterioration is not nearly as significant to an old stone wall's value as it is, say, to a nineteenth-century bronze sculpture or a colonial chest of drawers. Because most New England stone walls are practical, unpretentious creations, restoring them in practical, unpretentious ways amounts to a form of authenticity that is procedural as well as artistic. The restoration of a stone wall might best be understood in the sense expressed by Howard Mansfield, as imaginative renewal, not aesthetic mummification. By all means then, create fresh bases, fill interiors with riprap, and adjust dimensions; all with the primary objective of restoring the *purpose* and *presence* of the older wall rather than merely its original aspect.

We ourselves, after all, are historical actors in our own time, just as the wall builders we emulate were in theirs, and our efforts at renewing the work of the past will shortly be indistinguishable from that work. Even our finest re-creations will, in time, be candidates for restoration themselves. So, knock down the old gray walls. Because whether repairing or restoring, you have to dismantle first. And if a wall isn't historically unique and thus a candidate for embalming, it either deserves to be rebuilt soundly and practically or disassembled and used for its material. Either way, it undergoes "restoration."

An old wall is an object, but not quite in the same sense as an antique chair or a painted portrait. That is because in spite of its fixed, enduring appearance, a wall is actually a malleable aggregate, a collective, a temporary alliance of many small things that become, in their massed state, another thing entirely. A stone wall, then, is an idea as much as an object; an idea of barrier, or of line, of thickness, of age, of pattern, color, distance, order, or space. These concepts and others like them hold stone walls together as tightly as any amount of skilled craftsmanship, and they must also be restored, by means of a new application of craftsmanship itself, when the stones in the object begin to come apart. Journalist David Appell has likened New England's stone walls to "strings of rough pearls." Perhaps, then, a restored wall loses nothing more than pearls lose when, having spilled from a broken string, they are reassembled, reunited, on a new one.

SHAKER VILLAGE GATEPOST WITH UNRESTORED RETAINER
An old granite gatepost stands at the end of an unrestored field wall at Canterbury Shaker Village. The wall is constructed of split boulders closely fitted and laid on a batter. It is backed up, very roughly, with pickings from the hayfield to the left. (After a photograph by Scott Swank.)

WHY STONE WALLS ARE BEAUTIFUL 9

Ironically, the twice-despised stone of New England—baleful fieldstone and disruptive wall—is now the object of fierce affections. Traditionalists and developers both see in the weathered rock an eloquence and antique charm that speak to the heart.

—ERIC P. OLSEN, "A TAPESTRY OF STONE"

Something there is that dearly loves a wall.

—RONALD JAGER, *Last House on the Road*

ALONG THE EASTERN edge of the clearing in front of our house, there is an old stone wall. It marches agelessly out of the woods in a stolid line, its ranks of large, misshapen granite chunks perched together in a single thickness, like a column of proud, tired soldiers. There are gaps here and there, where some of the troops have fallen out, but the wall's line of march remains largely intact. Most of the stones wear the uniform of an old New England wall, a gray-green covering of lichen that softens their edges and surfaces with the worn and unmistakable patina of age.

This particular stretch of wall originates at a corner of the property almost a thousand feet down the hill from the house, and for more than half its length it is composed in classic single-stack farmer fashion, one stone thick and four to six stones high. But halfway along the clearing, just past an ancient, battered beech tree, the wall changes. Abruptly, it doubles and triples in thickness, and drops in height from three or four feet to two or two-and-a-half. Its stones are suddenly very much smaller, shrinking in average size from the bushel baskets of the single-stack to something closer to a cantaloupe or a human head. This section is also less carefully constructed, almost thrown together. Instead of a standing barrier, it is now a slumped and humble mound. After fifty feet, more or less, it ends, for no apparent reason. The land climbs quickly upward, and when it levels off the wall begins again, once more a standing single-stack but with fewer large chunks this time. It runs along like this for a hundred feet or so and changes once more, to a thicker, almost ground-level causeway of far smaller stones, perhaps on average the size of a baseball or an oversized muffin. At last the wall arrives at an opening where other walls converge, near the edge of a very old road now gone to trees. Here, it stops for good.

I don't know who built this wall, how long it took to assemble, or even whether it was done all at once or over several years. But I have no doubt that its layout and composition, its multiple personalities, are the result of a series of practical decisions made by the farmers who extracted a living from these hilly acres in the late eighteenth and early nineteenth centuries. I can even guess, with reasonable assurance, how the land in the immediate vicinity of its different sections was used. The great rising stretch from the bottom corner to the battered beech is clearly a livestock wall, built to contain sheep, most likely. When it was new, judging from its relatively intact sections and from the volume of fallen stone lying at its base, it was easily over four feet high. Furthermore, the wall does not contain any small stones, an indication that it was never used as a storage dump for rubble but only for pasture containment. The absence of smaller stones, either in the wall itself or a nearby mound, means this area of the land was never plowed or planted in any substantial or long-term way. A look around the forest floor on both sides of the wall confirms this view, for the area is still evenly pocked with large- and medium-sized protruding stones. This means my wall-building predecessors took what they needed to make their fence and simply left in place what they could not use.

This section's height and its heavy, single-stone composition indicate that it most likely stood on its own, without a cap of brush or wooden poles to augment it. But that is not the case farther up, where instead of a blocky single-stack, the wall becomes a lower, wider mound of smaller stones. Here was almost certainly a rail or brush fence, against and under which the stones were partly thrown and partly laid. There is some evidence in the way the stones are arranged that the outside lines of this wall were at least somewhat carefully composed, which means that the stonework was probably put in place first and later completed with more ephemeral materials. It is likely that some planting took place in this area, too, for although the wall itself does not contain enough very small stones to fully represent the annual pickings of a plowed field, there is a gully bank not far away where, underneath a few dozen generations of fallen leaves, lie the missing tons of fist-sized and smaller stones, scattered and absorbed into the bank almost invisibly.

The wall's abrupt, temporary termination just at the foot of the land's steep rise is a puzzlement. What happened here? Did the builders run out of nearby stone? Perhaps, but their willingness to transport large quantities to other sections of the wall argues against this theory, as does the gradual emergence of a base course of larger stones leading up the hill to the resumption of the single-stack. Perhaps this is a section that, for one reason or another, was simply never finished. We tend to assume that old New England stonework, whatever its present condition, was once complete, but this is not always correct. And my old wall offers another clue that hints at the possibility of incompletion: the presence, along much of its upper length, of numerous rusted strands of ancient barbed wire. If the sections of my wall built of smaller stones were originally topped with brush or rail fencing, as they almost certainly were, could not this now-vanished organic fence simply have continued up the hill, even before the builders had a chance to fill in its lower sections with collected stone? After 1874, when Joseph Glidden's patented improvements to barbed wire made Michael Kelly's 1868 invention widely popular, a great many busy farmers must have forsaken the laborious chore of stone wall building for the easy installation of wire fencing. By then, much of the sheep farming that so dominated New England's agricultural life in the early decades of the nineteenth century had given way to dairying, and cows are easily confined by barbed wire. If the original, temporary fence of brush or rail lasted into the era of wire, our farmers would no longer have had any practical reason to complete their stone wall.

Of course, old wire is difficult to date with much accuracy, but there is one more interesting detail to be observed along our wall. On its far upper end, where the smaller single-stack morphs once again into a collapsed stream of very small stones clearly picked from plowed acreage, there is the dead, dry stump of an American chestnut tree, hard against the edge of the wall's footprint. Two strands of barbed wire pass through its outer layers of slowly rotting wood, indicating that they were stapled to the tree when it was still alive and that it survived for a number of years afterward, long enough to absorb the wire to a depth of two inches or so. This detail would reveal very little if the stump were almost any other kind of tree, but the fact that it is a chestnut means a great deal, because this particular species, once among the most common and valuable in the eastern forest, was virtually annihilated in a mass fungal blight that began in 1904 and spread in all directions from its origination point in New York City. Chestnut blight reached central New England very quickly, so it's quite likely that the tree that left my wire-bearing stump died sometime in the mid-1920s or shortly thereafter. This means that the wire was probably strung not too long after the turn of the century, canceling the necessity to maintain, or even complete, more than sixteen hundred feet of variable stone wall that had almost certainly been standing for one hundred years or more even then.

I've built other walls here during the time we have lived on this land, but the one visitors always seem to notice is this one. It is crumbled, old, as common as clay, yet in spite of its condition, still alive somehow. Perhaps that is partly because its appearance constantly changes, from the black stubbornness of its half-buried persistence under heaps of snow to the startling blue-green glow it takes on after summer rains. Although there is nothing exceptional about this wall—whoever put it together was a good builder, but not a great one—I stare at it every day, thinking of all the things it is and of all the things it represents.

Why do so many people love New England's stone walls? What makes them "beautiful?" Why do we continue to build new ones and, increasingly, to defend and preserve the old ones that remain? My *Oxford English Dictionary*'s first entry under the word beauty reads, "That quality or combination of qualities which affords keen pleasure to the senses, esp. that of sight, or which charms the intellectual or moral faculties." If this is how we are to understand the meaning of beauty, then stone walls can claim the quality on every count.

The piling up of stones is a human activity ancient almost beyond calculation. Dry masonry belongs to every culture, in every part of the world where stones can be found. It is among the most primitive, practicable methods by which people organize their surroundings. After tens of thousands of years, it may be genetically or instinctually encoded in us, like our predispositions for language or art. "Entire millennia of human labors are known to us solely through their stone leavings," says Scott Sanders in his book about the limestone country of southern Indiana. "The only common stuff that rivals it for durability is language." So stone walls are beautiful because even when they are new, they are very, very old. Theirs is a beauty of continuity with the ordinary work of people throughout history.

Perhaps the impulse to build them is not even specifically human. Biologist Lewis Thomas noted that termites practice something very like wall building: "They place pellets atop pellets, then throw up columns and beautiful, curving, symmetrical arches, and the crystalline architecture of vaulted chambers is created." Thomas observed a kind of accumulating intelligence in termites, which flowers into masonry only after the colony reaches a certain population density, a certain level of development. Human stone piling may have begun as a practical response to need; for shelter or defense, to keep things in or out, or simply as an expression of presence, as guideposts or markers. One stone deliberately set on top of another performs the communicative function once identified by Kurt Vonnegut Jr.: It says, "I'm here." Another part of the beauty of stone walls, then, is a beauty of recognition, an approving response to signs that others have tried before us to resist entropy and inhabit the wildness of creation.

Stone walls are obvious signs of human activity, but they are also uniquely organic constructions, the result of nothing more invasive than the gathering and reorganizing of elements already present in the landscape. They are, in a way, equivalent to a bird's nest or a stickle-back's home at the bottom of a stream. Composed entirely of found natural objects, dry stone walls require nothing foreign, artificial, or processed. Virtually extruded from the earth itself, old stones, with their mosses and lichens, their rusty, blackened stains, their splashes of quartz or sparkling mica, settle into the changeable palette of the New England landscape with perfect ease, as comfortably as any meadow full of mayflowers or scarlet Judas tree. No other structures achieve their practical or aesthetic impact at such little cost to the environment. In fact, stone walls are themselves unique environments, hosting, protecting, and encouraging dozens of plant and animal species. So stone walls are beautiful as well for their simplicity and for their harmony, both visual and ecological, with the natural order.

The compositional virtues of stone walls are inherently appealing, but their beauty is enriched by broader layers of meaning, both artistic and psychological. It is hard to imagine, for example, how we would look at the New England countryside without them. The lines of a wall instruct our view, admonishing nature's exuberant indifference with a human touch that defines without despoiling. Stone walls give significance to space otherwise merely forested or cleared and create distinctions between one place and another, what the French philosopher Gaston Bachelard called "this side" and "beyond." In doing this, walls convey an almost primal impression of order and safety—even now, a sunny field seems much more securely tranquil if an enclosing wall separates it from the adjacent, darkened woods. Constructed of the hardest available material, stone walls nevertheless soften and civilize the land. At the same time, by responding to its form and flow, they reveal the qualities of a landscape with gentle, constant reminders of the harmony that is possible between the wild and the built environments. Even a stone wall's deteriorated remnants, unlike so much else that people leave behind, continue to satisfy the eye as pleasingly as any natural feature.

> Before it can ever be a repose for the senses, landscape is the work of the mind. Its scenery is built up as much from strata of memory as from layers of rock.
>
> — SIMON SCHAMA, *Landscape and Memory*

Stone walls are loved not just for their visual significance as objects, however, but also for their memorial associations. As a tangible legacy of bygone days, they put us in mind of bygone people, whose individual characters and attitudes we assess not in terms of direct experience but from the ruggedness, grace, and endurance we observe, or believe we observe, in their work. No stone wall looks like it was built by a slave, an indentured servant, or a weary child. Old walls seem instead to proclaim the past's industry and integrity, its faith and its diligence, its accomplishment in the face of harsh resistance. But the multiple symbolisms of stone walls derive from more than our careless inferences about their makers' sterling qualities or their actual identities. In many ways, our response to stone walls has to do with how we feel about ourselves.

We endow our forebears with a kind of innocence in our nostalgia for the evidence of their toil, as though their trials were somehow purer than our own and they themselves less complex human beings. At the same time, we find ourselves somehow unworthy of comparison with them, vaguely suspicious that we might not possess their resilient determination. Our admiration for their handiwork, then, is at least partly an expression of resentment for the elusiveness and confusion of modern life, and for the insubstantial nature of the work most of us now do. Perhaps we are pleased to believe in the past's particular brand of sufficiency because it instills hope in us that such a thing, having once existed, might one day be recaptured. Perhaps the beauty of that hope, even if only a daydream, is part of the beauty of an ancient wall.

But our appreciation for the ubiquitous stone subdivisions of the New England landscape is more subtle even than that. One reason we love walls, for instance, is that we no longer *have* to build them. Our freedom from the labor that wore their original creators down and drove many of them into the cities or the western territories is part of what the old walls memorialize. Their beauty, then, lies partly in their repose and in an implication of relief from arduousness that is, ironically, the opposite of former attitudes toward wall building. The competing imageries of a lost pastoral idyll and the backbreaking labor that made it possible enrich our perceptions of stone walls with paradox and a kind of mystery. "Everything comes alive when contradictions accumulate," observed Bachelard. Our responses to stone walls in the New England landscape are nothing if not contradictory and therefore animated in a way that encourages multiple, overlapping perceptions of their beauty.

> The great irony of this Herculean effort to clear the land and surround it with stone walls was that this pastoral landscape was exceedingly short lived. By 1840 the sheep farms were being abandoned in wholesale fashion. By 1900 more than half the cleared land was growing back to forest, shrouding thousands of miles of stone walls.
>
> — TOM WESSELS, *Reading the Forested Landscape*

Old walls are also beautiful because they are so sad. As historian David Lowenthal has pointed out, the presence in a place of substantial reliquary evidence of the past is often an indication that little has happened there in the intervening years. One reason we still have so much antique stonework to appreciate is that, in many rural areas especially, so little has come along to take its place. Our own age offers nothing remotely equivalent to the handmade creative energy lavished on the New England landscape by a few generations of eighteenth- and nineteenth-century wall builders. Their crumbling milldams, cow runs, and pasture walls are not just testaments to dogged craftsmanship, however, but also evidence of the eventual failure of their way of life.

In many New England places, like the Mink Hills of Warner, New Hampshire, the houses, fields, and even the roads of once thriving neighborhoods have been obliterated by time and the relentless forest, leaving nothing but what poet Donald Hall called "a community of cellar holes and stone doorsteps." Where the remains of old stonework are most common, they are the unmistakable record of an absence, all the more ironic because the "permanence" we see in them actually speaks of abandonment, futility, and regret. The nineteenth-century essayist Thomas Wentworth Higginson, who summered for many years among the exhausted old hill farms of Dublin, New Hampshire, expressed this sentiment in the first stanza of his poem "American Stonehenge":

> *Far up on these abandoned mountain farms*
> *Now drifting back to forest wilds again,*
> *The long, gray walls extend their clasping arms*
> *Pathetic monuments of vanished men.*

Higginson's verse, in contrast to more romantic characterizations of New England's original wall builders, speaks of ruin and wasted effort, not the glorious accomplishments of hardy pioneers. Today, his bitter elegy has softened to a lambent sadness that hovers over thousands of houseless foundations and sunken sheep enclosures, enhancing their beauty like a wistful breeze sighing in a pine grove.

About a hundred and sixty years ago, early in the Victorian age, the old way of seeing began to go out of American design. With it went the magic, and with the magic went the old feeling of being in a real place. Only a few specialists retained the creative gift that had once been commonplace . . .

—JONATHAN HALE, *The Old Way of Seeing*

Jonathan Hale's *The Old Way of Seeing* argues a controversial premise: that an intuitive, almost playful design sense once animated ordinary architectural practice, and that this sense is responsible for the qualities we most appreciate in certain old buildings, like many of the barns, churches, and colonial dwellings so central to our conception of the New England "place." Hale is quite specific about the date at which this intuitive design sense began to yield to a more self-conscious, symbol-displaying, "planned" approach. He traces the change to the onset of the Greek Revival, right around 1830, a year when the agricultural development of New England was very near its peak, and with it the most prolific period of dry stone construction. Among the reasons people give for loving old stone walls are their quirkiness, their patterns laced out upon the land, and the personal expression they see in the ways individual stones are laid against one another. These are precisely the attributes of Jonathan Hale's "old way of seeing," an intuition about what "looks right" that conforms, in his view, to singular yet universally resonant perceptions of pattern and proportion. That the old stonework revered by so many was largely built during Hale's halcyon period of common excellence in design is therefore no surprise.

With or without the assistance of architectural intuition, it is also arguable that many old stone walls are beautiful because they were meant to be. As early as the first decades of the nineteenth century, New England farmers began to subscribe to an agricultural aesthetic that promoted the marriage of convenience and beauty as "synonymous with excellence in farming and building." As Thomas Hubka demonstrates in his study of New England farm architecture, "The idea that function and beauty (or order) were inextricably united is one of the most fundamental tenets of a folk or vernacular value system. The ideal of beauty in the folk system is intrinsic to the work of everyday life and is never detached from that life." The deliberately dramatic siting of a stone wall along the edge of a ridge, for instance, or a high pasture wall whose cap runs precisely parallel to the rolling surface of a long stretch of meadow, eulogizes its builders as conscious sculptors, not at all indifferent to the possibility of gaining pleasure as well as utility from what they made. There is even a kind of humor in an old wall that climbs a slope too steep to stand on, or in one that features split boulders set upright or impossibly balanced three feet off the ground on much smaller stones.

"Illusion is an important element in the life of most Americans," journalist J. B. Harrison observed in 1890. Perhaps in the end, particularly now, stone walls are beautiful because they appear to be fixed things, always themselves no matter what alterations our own chaotic histories inflict on them. They are immune, in a way, to our illusions of the moment, and therefore the meanings they have gathered over time do not replace one another but simply accumulate as the generations pass, making them repositories of wisdom and memory, markers of every era they manage to survive. In this light, it seems appropriate not only to preserve the best of them, but also to create new ones. In its careful search for the meaning of this elastic word *beauty*, my *Oxford English Dictionary* goes on to quote Ralph Waldo Emerson, a New Englander who lived, as we do, in the daily presence of old stone walls. "We ascribe beauty to that which is simple," he says, "which has no superfluous parts; which exactly answers its end." What better definition of the beauty of stone walls could there be? It is impossible to return altogether to the ways of the past, and dishonest to regard only certain aspects of an era as embodiments of its entirety. Yet the simplicity and endurance of stone walls transcend culture and even history. The beauty we perceive in them is a reflection of our love for our own capacities and for our long life on this astonishing earth. Walls make us see the land. They make us see where we live. "Walking past a stone structure you've built yourself is a pleasure like no other," sums up stonemason and teacher David Reed.

Build one yourself. You'll see.

OUR GLOSSARY

COMMON AND UNCOMMON TERMS

Included here are both standard mason's terms and unique words coined by Owen and Associates.

BACKERS: An Owen term meaning stones unsuitable for use in the face of a wall; interior material.

BACKING UP: The task of laying stones behind the stones that compose the face of any wall.

BATTERING: A standard word for the building technique that slopes the face of a wall slightly inward as it rises. *Battered* retaining walls appear to lean backward into their banks; battered freestanding walls grow narrower as they rise, like A-frames.

BLOWOUT: Non-standard but recognized word for a localized, collapsed section of double-faced wall.

BUILDER: Any useful stone the size of a loaf of bread or larger that offers not only a presentable face, but also a shape that will lay solidly and cause few problems in subsequent courses.

BUTT ENDS: A standard term for squared-off, finished corners that terminate a freestanding wall without any additional support.

CAP: The conventional word for a wall's top layer of stones, no matter the style.

CAPSTONE: Another standard term for a relatively flat, relatively heavy stone used to finish off the top of a wall. Capstones lie flat on their broad sides, unlike *copestones*, which are laid in tight single rows, on edge.

CAT CAVE: Our phrase for a crack or opening between stones too large to be proportionately attractive in a given project; large enough, perhaps, for a cat to crawl inside.

CHEAP SEDUCER: A stone that glows with allure while it's on the ground, but can't be laid once hoisted to the wall. Our term.

CHINKING: A disreputable word (like *gyp* or *welsh*) for a dubious practice: that of stuffing or jamming small chips and fragments of stone (*chinkers*) into the cracks of a wall after it has been built. A standard word, unfortunately.

CIGARS, BASEBALLS, CANTALOUPES, ETC.: Examples of a group of object metaphors we use to indicate the particular shape of a stone we're looking for or are sick of dealing with. Others include dinner plates, Volkswagens, cannonballs, loaves-of-bread, and so on.

COPESTONE: See *Capstone*.

COURSE: Traditional word for a row of stones, bricks, or blocks running horizontally across the face of a project; more loosely, a layer.

DOUBLE-FACED WALL: The standard term for a freestanding wall or a section of a larger construction that shows laid faces on both sides.

EXPOSED: In descriptions of stone steps, our term for those which are not built into retaining or other walls, but consist only of the step-stones themselves. In carpentry, also known as *open* stairs.

FACE: That part of a wall or of any individual stone in it that shows itself to the outside world. A standard term.

FARMER WALL: Loosely, one of several common terms for informal or rough stone walls, usually just one or two stones thick. (See also *Single-stack walls*.)

FOOTPRINT: Our adaptation of a word to mean the area of ground on which a wall actually stands.

FREESTANDING WALL: The standard term for a wall that supports itself in space without being built into a bank or laterally attached to any other structure.

GRANITE: A common type of igneous rock largely composed of quartz, feldspar, and mica that can occur in shades of gray, black, green, white, pink, and yellow.

GRANITE KISS: That instantly discouraging, and inevitable, experience in stone work when a fingertip or two fails to escape the contact point between two large stones on the occasion of their first meeting. An Owen invention, dearly earned.

HARD CAP: Our term for a finishing layer of large, relatively flat stones placed along the top of a wall.

LEADING EDGE: On steps, a common term for the outer, exposed ends of step-stones, where the *rise* meets the *run* on each successive *tread* (see these terms below).

LIFT: In masonry, a common noun meaning the height of a given course of stones, brick, block, or concrete.

MOSSLGRO: The Owen brand name for a mysterious or apocryphal substance reputed to encourage the growth of moss and lichen on freshly laid stone. Included are buttermilk, horse urine, molasses, manure tea, etc.

PLANE WINDOW: Our phrase for the space between an imaginary pair of parallel lines, used to define the relative roughness of the face shown by a given wall.

PLUMB: A common term for (1) Straight up and down, vertical; or (2) To build or adjust a thing so that it stands vertically.

PROBLEMSOLVER: A small stone or oddly shaped shard, often an elongated triangle, that fits snugly into a space between larger stones too narrow or irregularly defined to admit an ordinary builder. More Owen shorthand.

PROFILE: Standard term for light wooden frames built to the planned horizontal and vertical dimensions of a wall's ends, and set in place as anchors for the strings that guide builders during construction.

PUDDLE CAP: Our term for a finishing layer of small stones.

RETAINING WALL: Traditional name for a wall with only one visible face, built against an earthen bank or some other abrupt change in grade or topography.

RETURNS: Our adaptation of a carpenter's term, which we use to mean the containing side-walls of a stairway, or any short, finishing section of retaining wall that disappears into a higher grade.

RIPRAP: Another (standard) term for crushed granite, usually of larger size (six or more inches), which is extremely useful as backing for retaining walls.

RISE: Standard word for the height of a step.

ROD, OR PERCH: Old words for an old system. A rod (also called a *perch* or a *pole*) is a length of 16½ feet, derived from a measuring device called a Gunter's Chain, which is four rods, or 66 feet, long. Since its invention in 1620, the chain has defined the way land is measured. One acre, for instance, is an area of 10 square chains, or 43,560 square feet. One mile is a distance of eighty chains, or 5,280 feet.

RUN: In stairway building, a standard word for the depth of an individual step, or for the horizontal distance traveled by the entire stairway.

SANDSTONE: A sedimentary rock that is relatively soft and light, and has a gritty, abrasive surface.

SHALE: A sedimentary rock that is made of compressed mud or clay and is relatively easy to split into thin layers.

SHIMMING: The use of shards, chips, fragments, or flat stones to stabilize the placements of larger builders or step-stones during construction. Shims are different from chinkers because they are installed as part of a wall's structure during assembly, not later as fill for gaps and cracks.

SINGLE-STACK WALL: A rough freestanding wall, one stone thick.

SKI JUMP: Our pejorative term for a stone laid so that its upper surface slopes out and down, making secure placement of one or more stones on top of it impossible.

SNOUT: A traditional word for the point on an exposed stone that projects farthest out from the face of the wall.

SPALLS: A standard mason's term for stone chips or splinters used to shim or stabilize larger builders within a wall.

STACK BONDING: The incorrect placement of stones of similar size one directly on top of another, so that long vertical cracks (see *vertical running joints*) develop in the wall face and extend through several courses. A standard term.

STEP-STONES: Common term for the shapely, cooperative stones that form the actual treads of stairways. From it we have derived *step-mates*, meaning step-stones that fit closely together side by side in treads that require more than one stone.

THROUGH-STONE: A traditional word for a long, binding stone that passes through the entire width of a freestanding wall, often protruding on one or both sides. Uncommon in New England due to their scarcity, through-stones are used extensively in the British Isles, and in other parts of the United States, such as Kentucky.

THRUFTER: Derek's coinage for a stone that, in addition to having a usable face, also has enough length to be laid so that it reaches deep into the mass of wall behind the face, trapping itself and helping to stabilize the section all around it. Good thrufters are generally at least eighteen inches to two feet long. The term derives from a wry misreading of an eighteenth-century document—it really means "thruster."

TOWN POUND: Traditional designation for a structure for the confinement of stray animals; usually square, often about 30 by 30 feet, with heavy walls six feet or more high. Town pounds were built by thousands of New England communities in the eighteenth and nineteenth centuries, and many are still standing.

TRAPPING: Our word for the technique of gripping relatively shallow stones in the face of a wall by laying longer builders around or above them, or of laying the shallow stones so that their wider ends are solidly encased within the mass of stone.

TREAD: Standard term for the surface of a step on which one stands, or for the entire width of the step.

TRENCHING: The Owen builders adapted this word to mean the practice of creating a stable base for a wall by excavating a trench, slightly wider than the wall itself, and filling it with stony material like riprap.

VERTICAL RUNNING JOINTS: Uninterrupted cracks between stones that pass straight up through several courses.

BIBLIOGRAPHY

Allport, Susan. *Sermons in Stone: The Stone Walls of New England and New York.* New York and London: W. W. Norton, 1990.

Appell, David. "Living Walls." Feature article in *Audubon* 101, no. 1 (January/February 1999): 72.

Arnold, Bob. *On Stone: A Builder's Notebook.* Boston: Origin Press, 1998.

Bachelard, Gaston. *The Poetics of Space.* Boston: Beacon Press, 1969.

Barron, Hal S. *Those Who Stayed Behind: Rural Society in Nineteenth Century New England.* Cambridge, England, New York, and Melbourne, Australia: Cambridge University Press, 1984.

Brown, Dona. *Inventing New England: Regional Tourism in the Nineteenth Century.* Washington and London: Smithsonian Institution Press, 1995.

Carter, Jeff. *Stout Hearts and Leathery Hands.* London: Angus and Robertson; Adelaide, Australia: Rigby Limited, 1968.

Conniff, Richard, and Alen MacWeeney. *Irish Walls*. New York: Stewart, Tabori, and Chang, 1986.

Cramb, Ian. *The Art of the Stonemason*. Cincinnati: Betterway Books, 1992.

Cronon, William. *Changes in the Land: Indians, Colonists, and the Ecology of New England*. New York: Hill and Wang, 1983.

Crowe, Norman. *Nature and the Idea of a Man-Made World*. Cambridge, Mass., and London: The MIT Press, 1995.

Dickinson, Emily. "The products of my farm are these," in *Emily Dickinson* (Laurel Poetry Series). New York: Dell, 1960.

Edwards, Betty. *Drawing on the Right Side of the Brain*. Los Angeles: J. P. Tarcher/Putnam, 1979.

Farren, Robert. "The Mason," in *The Mentor Book of Irish Poetry*. New York: New American Library, 1965.

Fields, Curtis P. *The Forgotten Art of Building a Stone Wall*. Dublin, N.H.: Yankee Inc., 1971.

Foster, David R. *Thoreau's Country: Journey Through a Transformed Landscape*. Cambridge, Mass., and London: Harvard University Press, 1999.

Frost, Robert. "A Star in a Stone-Boat," in *Selected Poems*. New York: Holt, Rinehart and Winston, 1963.

Garner, Lawrence. *Dry Stone Walls*. Princes Risborough, Buckinghamshire, England: Shire Publications Ltd., 1984.

Goldsworthy, Andy. *Wall*. New York: Harry N. Abrams, 2000.

Hale, Jonathan. *The Old Way of Seeing*. Boston and New York: Houghton Mifflin, 1994.

Harrison, J. B. "The Abandoned Farms of New Hampshire," *The Granite Monthly* (Concord, N.H.) 3, nos. 5, 6 (June 1890).

Hastings, Scott E. *The Last Yankees: Folkways in Eastern Vermont and the Border Country*. Hanover, N.H., and London: University Press of New England, 1990.

Hayward, Gordon. "Rubble Raiser." Feature article in *Country Journal* 27, no. 2 (March/April 2000).

Hesiod. *Theogeny, Works and Days, Shield*. Translated by Apostolos N. Athanassakis. Baltimore and London: Johns Hopkins University Press, 1983.

Hubka, Thomas C. *Big House, Little House, Back House, Barn: The Connected Farm Buildings of New England*. Hanover, N.H., and London: University Press of New England, 1984.

Jackson, J. B. *The Necessity for Ruins (And Other Topics)*. Amherst, Mass.: University of Massachusetts Press, 1980.

Jager, Ronald. *Last House on the Road: Excursions into a Rural Past*. Beacon Press, Boston, 1994.

Jerome, John. *Stone Work*. Hanover, N.H.: University Press of New England, 1996.

Lord, Charles Chase. *Life and Times in Hopkinton, N.H.* Concord, N.H.:

Republican Press Association, 1890; facsimile edition, Portsmouth, N.H.: New Hampshire Antiquarian Society, Peter Randall Publisher, 1991.

Lowenthal, David. *The Past Is a Foreign Country*. Cambridge, England, New York, and Melbourne, Australia: Cambridge University Press, 1985.

Mansfield, Howard. *In The Memory House*. Golden, Colo.: Fulcrum, 1993.

———. *The Same Ax, Twice: Restoration and Renewal in a Throwaway Age*. Hanover, N.H.: University Press of New England, 2000.

Martin, George A. *Fences, Gates and Bridges: A Practical Manual*. New York: O. Judd, 1887; Chambersburg, Pa.: Alan C. Hood & Co., 1992.

McAfee, Patrick. *Irish Stone Walls*. Dublin: The O'Brien Press, 1997.

McRaven, Charles. *Building with Stone*. Pownal, Vt.: Storey Books, 1989.

Murray-Wooley, Carolyn, and Karl Raitz. *Rock Fences of the Bluegrass*. Lexington, Ky.: University Press of Kentucky, 1992.

Nelson, Florence Agnes. *Lest We Forget: Sketches of Rural New England in the 19th Century*. Portland, Maine: Falmouth Publishing House, 1949.

Olsen, Eric P. "A Tapestry of Stone: The Rock Walls of New England." Feature article in *The World and I* (Washington Times Publication) 13, no. 6 (June 1998): 196.

Rainsford-Hannay, Frederick. *Dry Stone Walling*. London: Faber and Faber, 1957.

Sanders, Scott R. *Stone Country*. Bloomington, Ind.: Indiana University Press, 1985.

Schama, Simon. *Landscape and Memory.* New York: Vintage Books, 1996.

Schmid, Richard. *Alla Prima: Everything I Know about Painting.* Stove Prairie, Colo.: Stove Prairie Press, 1998.

Shepheard, Paul. *The Cultivated Wilderness; or, What Is Landscape?* Graham Foundation for Advanced Studies in the Fine Arts, Chicago; and Cambridge, Mass., and London: The MIT Press, 1997.

Sloane, Eric. *Diary of an Early American Boy.* New York: Funk and Wagnalls, 1962.

———— *Our Vanishing Landscape.* New York and Toronto: New York: Funk and Wagnalls, 1955; Ballantine Books/Random House, 1974.

Spirn, Anne Whiston. *The Language of Landscape.* New Haven and London: Yale University Press, 1998.

Stilgoe, John R. *Common Landscape of America, 1580–1845.* New Haven and London: Yale University Press, 1982.

Thomas, Lewis. "On Societies As Organisms," in *The Lives of a Cell.* New York: Viking, 1974.

Thomson, Betty Flanders. *The Changing Face of New England.* New York: The Macmillan Company, 1958.

Thorson, Kristine, and Robert Thorson. *Stone Wall Secrets.* Gardiner, Maine: Tilbury House, 1998.

Truettner, William H., and Roger B. Stein, eds. *Picturing Old New England: Image and Memory.* New Haven and London: National Museum of American Art, Smithsonian Institution/Yale University Press, 1999.

Vivian, John. *Building Stone Walls*. Pownal, Vt.: Storey Books/Garden Way Publishing, 1976.

Wessels, Tom. *Reading the Forested Landscape: A Natural History of New England*. Woodstock, Vt.: The Countryman Press, 1997.

Wood, Pamela, ed. *The Salt Book*. Garden City, N.Y.: Anchor Press/Doubleday, 1977 (out of print).

INDEX

Page numbers in italics indicate illustrations.

A

B

C

U

V

W